Copyright © 2006 by Joan Few, 3rd Edition, June 2007

ISBN 0-9785875-0-2

All rights reserved. No part of this publication may be reproduced or transmitted in any form or by any means, electronic or mechanical, including photocopy, recording or any information storage and retrieval system without permission in writing from the publisher.

Published in the United States by Few Publications, 700 Hill Street, Gold Hill, Colorado 80302, (http://web.mac.com/joan_few)

Printed by Lightning Source Inc., 1246 Heil Quaker Blvd., La Vergne, TN 37086

The cover photograph of the Main House at the Lake Jackson Plantation, taken in 1890's, is used courtesy of the Brazoria County Historical Commission.

Sugar, Planters, Slaves and Convicts

The History and Archaeology

of

The Lake Jackson Plantation

Brazoria County, Texas

Joan Few

Table of Contents

Introduction

Acknowledgments

I.	Why Sugar? Why Texas?	1.
	Soil Types of Brazoria County, Texas	4.
	Antebellum Plantations of Brazoria County, Texas	6.
II.	"STRIKE": The Production of Granulated sugar in antebellum Texas	9.
	Train of Sugar Evaporation kettles	14.
	Sugar Production 1852-1858	18.
III.	The Abner and Margaret Jackson Family, Brazoria County, Texas	21.
	Aerial Photo of Lake Jackson Plantation	27.
	Map Showing the 7 Tracts of the Lake Jackson Plantation	28.
	Map Showing Three Jackson Plantations	35.
IV.	Family Tragedy: The Probate Years (1861-1873)	41.
V.	Died in the A.M., Buried in the P.M.: Slave Life in the Lower Brazos River Valley	67.
	Table 1, Slave Populations	69.
	Table 2, Slave Holders	70.
	Table 3, Major Planters	70.
	Table 4, Slaves by Sex & Age at Lake Jackson	75.
	Table 5, Lake Jackson Sugar Production	78.
VI.	Juneteenth and Beyond	85.
	Wages Between July and December, 1865	86.
	List of Payments to Black Hands	91.
VII.	The Convict Lease System in Texas and the Use of Convicts at Lake Jackson Plantation	97.
VIII.	Excavating Nineteenth Century Sugar Mills	107.
	Photo, Indian Church Mill, Belize	109.
	Photo, Osceola Boiler and Chimney	110.
	Photo, Osceola Foundations	111.
	Photo, Firebox at Osceola	112.
	Photo, Flue Chimney at Osceola	113.
	Floor Plan, Osceola Sugar Mill	114.
	Photos, Lake Jackson Mill	115.
	Photo, Copper Sieve	118.
	Photo of Kettle Setting	119.

	Foundations of Lake Jackson Sugar Mill	119.
	Photo of Lake Jackson Sugar Mill	120.
	Photo of Convict Construction	123.
	Photo of Lake Jackson Mill	125.
	Photo of Convict Boiler Foundation	126.
	Photo of Convict Period Alterations	127.
	Drawing of Jackson - Convict Mill Changes	128.
	Photo of Historical Profile	129.
	Drawing of Four Nineteenth Century Sugar Mills	131.
	Photos of Sugar Mill Excavations	132.
IX.	Excavation of the Lake Jackson Plantation Main House and Associated Structures	133.
	Artifact Types at Lake Jackson	135.
	Artifact Types by Structures	136.
	Structures at Lake Jackson	137.
	Photo and Drawing of Main House	139.
	Front Porch, Main House	140.
	Photo of Artifacts	143.
	Drawing of Structure A	144.
	Drawing of Structure B	146.
	Structure B Artifacts	149.
	Photo of Structure B	150.
	Photo and Drawing of Structure C	151.
	Drawing of Structure D	153.
	Structure D. Provenanced Artifacts	154.
	Chart, Comparison of Rooms A & D, Structure D	156.
X.	Summary	157.
XI.	Appendices:	
	Chapter 2: Sugar Production by Plantations between 1852 and 1858	163.
	Chapter 3: Letter from James Reed to James F. Perry, May 4, 1846	169.
	Letters from James Hamilton to James Perry	
	Marriage Contract between Abner Jackson and Sarah Brownlee, 1860	
	Chapter 4: July 1, 1862 Inventory by John C. Jackson of the estate of Abner Jackson including community property	172.
	Chapter 5: Yearly slave work schedules by month	180.
	Chapter 6: List of monetary transactions of Freedmen and women on the Darrington plantation in 1866	188.

Introduction

Archaeologists and historians both look for information about the past; they just use different tools and methods to do their research. Historical archaeology has the advantage of combining both avenues of research to create a more complete story.

As an archaeologist, I am frequently asked, "What is the most exciting 'thing' that you have ever found." The excitement is not in finding the "thing," but discovering what the "thing" can tell us about the past. Every artifact has information, and if it is found where it was used and in association with other artifacts that were used during the same period, that information is enhanced.

After excavation, the real challenge in archaeology begins. All artifacts are analyzed in many different ways until they begin to form patterns, like pieces of a jigsaw puzzle falling into place to form a picture. Through artifacts we can look into the past.

This book represents nine years of combined archaeological and historical research to form a more complete story of this part of Texas that was known in the Nineteenth Century as the "Sugar Bowl." It also explains how archaeologists work and how archaeological research provides information.

Our archaeological site is the Lake Jackson Plantation, a State Archeological Landmark[1] (41BO172[2]). This 2.719 acre site is a small portion of a nineteenth century sugar and cotton plantation, but it contains the major structures of the plantation and hundreds of years of history starting with the Indians who camped there. Our focus will be on the sugar plantations that used slave labor before the Civil War and convict labor after the Civil War.

The Lake Jackson SAL plantation buildings were destroyed in the great hurricane of 1900 that devastated Galveston, Texas. After 1900 cattle grazed on the property until 1945 when Dow Chemical Company constructed a park that was used by its employees and the public. In 1992 the land was transferred to the Lake Jackson Historical Association and they turned the site into the Lake Jackson Plantation historic park.

Our archaeological and historical research provides information on the operations of the Lake Jackson Plantation; family life; the Antebellum sugar industry and technological transitions in the nineteenth sugar industry, which are visible in the altered structure of the sugar mill; information about the everyday life of the slaves; insights into the "slavery to freedom" transition period; and the appalling conditions of convict life in Texas in the nineteenth century.

---

[1] Brazosport Archaeological Society, 1989, Historical Resource Survey of The Lake Jakcson Plantation, Survey Report 89-01. BAS Publication, 400 College Drive, Lake Jackson, Texas 77566

[2] 41BO172 is the site trinomial: 41 = Texas, BO = Brazoria County, and 172 is the Brazoria County site number. This system is used throughout the U.S.

Acknowledgments

Dow Chemical saved an important historical site when they made the Lake Jackson Plantation into a recreational park and fenced off the major structures for preservation. They transferred ownership to the Lake Jackson Historical Association who have made the site into a historic park open to the public.

The Lake Jackson Plantation became a State Archeological Landmark (SAL) because of the diligent efforts of members of the Brazosport Archaeological Society. The initial research on the site was done by Sue Gross, Chris D. Kneupper, Johnney T. Pollan, Sandra D. Pollan, James L. Smith, Judy S. Wayland and David J. Wayland.[3]

The contributions of hundreds of people, who volunteered to assist with the archeological excavations, have made this research possible and include archaeology students from the University of Houston Clear Lake (UHCL), members of the Texas Archeological Society (TAS), the Brazosport Archaeological Society(BAS), and the Houston Archeological Society (HAS). Ninety percent of the archaeological work accomplished was during the 1994 and 1995 TAS Field Schools held at the site. The Brazosport Archaeological Society was pivotal to both TAS Field Schools; society members dedicated three years to this effort. Johnney Pollan was responsible for local arrangements; Sue Gross, registrar; Chris D. Kneupper, programs; and Sandra Pollan curated all artifacts. Juliann Pool (on loan from the Texas Parks and Wildlife Department) was lab director; Anne Fox, University of Texas at San Antonio; Pat Mercado-Allinger, State Archeologist; and Robbie Brewington, Texas A & M University and UHCL, served as area supervisors. Photographers were Sherri Avery, Joanne Ancira, Elvis Allen, and Raymond Blackstone. Field secretaries were Vicki Hatfield, Karen Acker, Marcy Grubbs, and Velicia Hubbard. Members of the Houston Archeological Society under the leadership of Sheldon Kendall and Dick Gregg contributed many hours of logistical and manual support.

The productivity of the field schools was enhanced by the many volunteers from BAS, HAS, and TAS who spent many weeks in the spring of 1994, clearing overburden from the site.

---

[3] Brazosport Archaeological Society, 1989, Historical Resource Survey of The Lake Jackson Plantation, Survey Report 89-01. BAS Publication, 400 College Drive, Lake Jackson, Texas 77566

Artifacts analysis was by: Karen Elliott Fustes, Indian ceramics; Sandra D. Pollan, historic ceramics; Juliann Pool, buttons; and William L. McClure, bone. Barbara Butler (UHCL) served as administrative secretary and UHCL coordinator for both field schools. This author is deeply indebted to the encouragement and professional support given by Dr. Mary G. Hodge (1946-1996) to the Lake Jackson State Archeological Landmark Site research program.

Robert Armstrong, an expert on sugar production and former President of Imperial Sugar, Sugarland, Texas, was a generous mentor in guiding this author in an understanding of the nineteenth century sugar process and identifying the best researchers and scholars of that period.

The archeological excavations were permitted and assisted by the owners of the site, the Lake Jackson Historical Association. Mac McClure, Harry Sargent, Vic Vickers, and Gary Vickers were vital to the success of this research. The many members of the Association who serve as docents to the site, make site visitations possible for the public. The site is located on Hwy 2004, one half mile west of Hwy 288, in the city limits of Lake Jackson.

The Lake Jackson Historical Museum (249 Circle Way - www.lakejacsonmuseum.org) has an interpretive history of the plantation with some artifacts on display. Artifacts and records are curated at the Museum.

The excavations were assisted by the University of Houston Clear Lake, who allowed classes in historical archeology and archeological field methods to be taught at the site. Dow Chemical Company provided to the TAS Field Schools; porta-potties, expenses for special guest speakers, bus tours for TAS members, buses for field trips for the children's program, and permission to excavate and assistance with the Follet Lake prehistoric site. The City of Lake Jackson allowed the Field Schools to use Dunbar Park for camping, the free use of the Dunbar Pavilion, installed water lines into the camp area, installed shower tie-ins to the city sewer system and arranged for garbage pickup. Brazosport College provided space for the archeological laboratory. Brazosport Museum of Natural Science provided storage for the artifacts which numbered 78,782. The Lake Jackson Lake Association gave permission to perform underwater studies in Lake Jackson. The Texas Archeological Research Laboratory provided the equipment and personnel to operate the Total-Station to generate topographical

maps of the Follet Lake site. The Lake Jackson Chamber of Commerce and the Lake Jackson Tourists Bureau provided promotion and assistance.

Kelso Vernor Material and Equipment donated the use of their heavy equipment and their operator, Gary Funderburk, who expertly removed the old Dow Chemical Co. road that was covering some of the ruins at the site.

We are very grateful to Margaret F. McDonald for sharing the Plantation Journal of the H.G. Shrock Plantation in Wharton, County. The Journal is a wealth of information about slave life along the Brazos River.

I am sorry that space will not permit the naming of the almost 1,000 volunteers who participated in the excavations. Each contribution to Texas history is deeply appreciated.

Special thanks to James Smith, Diane Baird and Jo K. Horan for identifying needed changes in editions 1 and 2.

Additional Sources

A podcast (http://web.mac.com/joan_few) accompanies this book and contains additional pictures, information, and discussions of each chapter.

For more pictures and information on the 1994 and 1995 Texas Archeological Society Field Schools, visit the web site, Texas Beyond History, and click on Lake Jackson.

"Raisin Cane" is a three part video about the site and the Texas Sugar Industry. Produced by Garfield Video Productions, detailed information about the videos and order information can be found at www.anth.ucab.edu/videos/raisincane.html. Contact information at garfieldvideo@yahoo.com, 512-247-2395.

Visit The Society of American Archaeology (www.saa.org) website for information about professional archaeologists, sites, and public education.

To Arthur,
For his many years of encouragement
and support.

Why Sugar? Why Texas?

Sugar cane is not indigenous to the Americas; its origins lie somewhere in Southeast Asia. Christopher Columbus brought sugar cane to the Caribbean on his second voyage and established a plantation on Santo Domingo, which is now the Dominican Republic. The first sugar mill in the Americas was built in 1508 in the village of Isabela. Hernando Cortes transported sugar cane to Mexico and established two plantations. From the Caribbean and Mexico, the cultivation of sugar cane spread to Brazil, Peru, and Argentina.[1] As sugar cane plantations grew, so did the demand for slave labor.[2] By the mid-1600's tropical America had become the greatest sugar-producing area in the world.[3] In response to this development, slaves exported from Africa quintupled to an estimated total of 1,341,000 in the seventeenth century.[4]

In the early 1700s Pierre LeMoyne Iberville journeyed up a small bayou near Lake Pontchartrain, with sixty men. He found a deserted Indian village where he planted seed cane brought from Santo Domingo. This venture was not successful; however, the next attempt was. Jesuits in Santo Domingo sent seed cane to Jesuits in Louisiana in 1751 along with several Negroes who knew how to grow the plant.[5] From this planting sugar cane became a major crop in Louisiana. By 1823, sugar production in Louisiana had reached 30,000 hogsheads[6], or approximately 30,000,000 pounds of crystallized sugar a year. The success of sugar production in Louisiana inspired the introduction of sugar cane into Texas.

---

[1] Pennington, N.L. 1977 "Sugar" *The World Book Encyclopedia,* Vol. 18, Page 768
[2] Wolf, E.R. 1982, *Europe and the People Without History,* University of California Press
[3] Pennington, 1977
[4] Wolf 1977: Page 195
[5] Johnson, W.E. 1961 *A Short History Of The Sugar Industry in Texas,* Texas Gulf Coast Historical Association Publications, Vol 4 #1, April, Page 7
[6] Ibid, Page 8

Around the world the demand for sugar was growing; partly due to the increased availability of tea and coffee on the world market. In England in 1700 the quantity of sugar consumed was approximately 10,000 tons. By 1790 consumption had increased to 81,000 tons. By 1860, the annual consumption of sugar was about 38 pounds per person in England and in the United States it was over 40 pounds per person.[7] This demand fueled the production of sugar in Texas.

In 1820 Moses Austin stated to the Spanish Governor at San Antonio, Texas, that, "It was his intention to provide for his subsistence by raising sugar and cotton,"[8] in Spanish Texas. The Spanish Governor must have been aware that sugar cane would grow in Texas because a sugar mill had been established at the Mission San José y San Miguel de Aguayo in San Antonio by 1755.[9] Moses Austin was successful in convincing the Spanish Governor that the colonization of Texas would be profitable for Spain, and he received a Royal Commission to be Texas' first Impresario and to bring three hundred families to Texas. Austin returned home to Missouri and died soon after his return. His son, Stephen, agreed to carry on the impresario grant.

Stephen Austin traveled to Natchitoches in Louisiana where he met with Spanish Commissioners who acknowledged him as heir to his father's grant.[10] Austin was allowed to survey the country and choose a site for his colony. He searched Texas between Nacogdoches to

---

[7] British Encyclopedia, 1860, London Vol.20 (S), Page 334. By comparison, the annual consumption of natural sweeteners (sugar, corn sweeteners, syrup and honey) in the United States in 1997 was 154 pounds per person per year, according to the april 2000 USDA Agricultural Outlook.

[8] Creighton, J.A. 1975 *A Narrative History of Brazoria County.* Brazoria county Historical Commission, Page 196.

[9] Clark, J.W. Jr. 1976 The Sugar Industry at Mission San Jose' Y San Miguel De Aguayo, *Bulletin of the Texas Archeological Society,* Vol. 47, Austin, Texas Page 245

[10] Fehrenbach, T.R. 1968 *Lone Star: A History of Texas and the Texans,* The Macmillan Company, Page 136

the east and San Antonio to the west. Austin claimed the land south of the Camino Real[11] lying between the Colorado and the Brazos Rivers.[12]

Austin's colonists began to arrive in Texas in 1821;[13] many bringing their slaves with them to provide labor for sugar and cotton production. The Spanish Government sometimes tolerated slavery and sometimes prohibited it. The Texas colonists simply ignored the Spanish Government.[14]

The settlers in the colony recognized three types of soil in Brazoria County: peach land, considered the finest; cane land, very rich; and prairie land.[15] Peach land was identified by the presence of the wild peach tree, sometimes called the cherry laurel, and the cane land by dense stands of hardwood trees. In current soil surveys the peach soils are called Asa-Norwood soil (type 4), which are loamy, well drained, moderately permeable soils found on bottom lands. The cane lands are called Pledger-Brazoria soils (type 2). They are clayey, somewhat poorly drained, very slowly permeable soils also found on bottom lands.[16] The prairie land refers to land on the coastal terraces such as Lake Charles soil (type 1), Bernard-Edna soil (type 3), and Edna-Aris soil (type 4), where tall prairie grass will grow along with dense stands of hardwood trees, stands of mixed hardwoods, or mixed stands of pine and hardwood trees.

---

[11] Spanish Road between San Antonio and Nacogdoches, Texas
[12] Farenbach, 1968 Page 137
[13] Ibid, Page 138
[14] Ibid, Page 165
[15] Platter, A.A. 1961 *Education, Social and Economic Characteristics of the Plantation Culture of Brazoria County, Texas.* Ph.D. Dissertation, Department of Education, University of Houston Houston, Texas, Page 4
[16] Soil Survey of Brazoria County, 1981 United States Department of Agriculture, Soil Conservation Service in Cooperation with the Brazoria County Commissioners Court and Agricultural Experimental Station. Page 5

Soil Types of Brazoria County, Texas

1. Lake Charles, 2. Pledger-Brazoria, 3. Bernard-Edna, 4. Asa Norwood, 5. Edna-Aris

Brazoria, Fort Bend, Wharton, and Matagorda Counties had the best land for growing sugar cane and the growing season was long enough to allow the cane to mature sufficiently for the extraction of sugar. North of these counties the growing season was too short, and the cane would yield juice too low in saccharin [sucrose] content to produce sugar.[17]

As the plantations of Brazoria County were developed, the planters were guided by two priorities: (1) water for transportation and (2) acquisition of the best lands, peach and cane. All the plantations have access either to the Brazos River, Oyster Creek, or the San Bernard River. Some, such as the Lake Jackson plantation, had access to two waterways. The plantations included as much peach and cane soil as possible and some prairie land for cattle grazing. Stephen Austin knew exactly what he was looking for when he chose this land to establish his colony.

By 1828 sugar was growing in Texas, and Texans were producing between sixty to eighty hogsheads [barrels containing about one thousand pounds of crystallized sugar] per year, and by 1829, 140 hogsheads.[18] Texas and sugar were a natural combination in the Nineteenth Century in the Brazos River Valley. Sugar cane is no longer grown commercially along the Brazos River.

http://web.mac.com/joan_few

---

[17] Ibid, Pages 9-38
[18] Johnson, 1961, Page 11

Antebellum Plantations of Brazoria County[19]

1. Bingham - Francis Bingham	2. Darrington - Sterling McNeel, Abner Jackson	3. Willow Glen
4. Coffee	5. Compton	6. George A. Smith
7. Tankersly	8. China Grove - Albert Sidney Johnson	9. Palo Alto
10. Quarl's	11. Drayton	12. Orozimbo - Dr. James A. E. Phelps
13. Waverly - William Kennedy	14. Chenango - Monroe Edwards - Colonel W. Sharp	15. Peach Lake Judge R. J. Townes, later Van
16. Maner	17. Osceola - William and Eliza Westall Austin Hill	18. Waldeck - Morgan L. Smith
19. Patton - Became Varner-Hogg Plantation	20. Josiah H. Bell	21. Bynum - Robert and David G. Mills
22. Cedar Grove	23. John Sweeny	24. Retrieve - Jacksons and James Hamilton
25. T. G. Masterson	26. Spencer	27. Strayton
28. Levi Jordan and James C. McNeill	29. Mims - Sarah Mims	30. A. Winston
31. Christopher Bell	32. Lake Jackson - Abner and Margaret Jackson	33. Eagle Island - William and Sarah Ann Groce Wharton
34. M. A. Bryan	35. Evergreen Calvit - Mrs. B. M. Calvit	36. Jack Place

---

[19] Texas Parks and Wildlife Department, 1983 *Preservation Plan and Program for Varner-Hogg Plantation State Historical Park, Brazoria county, Texas.* Vol. I & II. Historic Sites & Restoration Branch, Texas Parks & Wildlife Department, TPWD 4000-293, Austin, Texas, Adapted from Platter, 1961

37. Oakland - James P. Caldwell	38. Crosby - Thomas P. and Clementine Crosby	39. Pleasant Grove - Leader McNeel
40. Munson - Henry and Ann Munson	41. A. E. Westall	42. Ellerslie - John Greenville McNeel
43. Hawkins	44. Peach Point - James F. and Emily Austin Perry	45. Durazno - William Joel and Lavinia Perry Bryan

Brazoria County Antebellum Plantations[20]

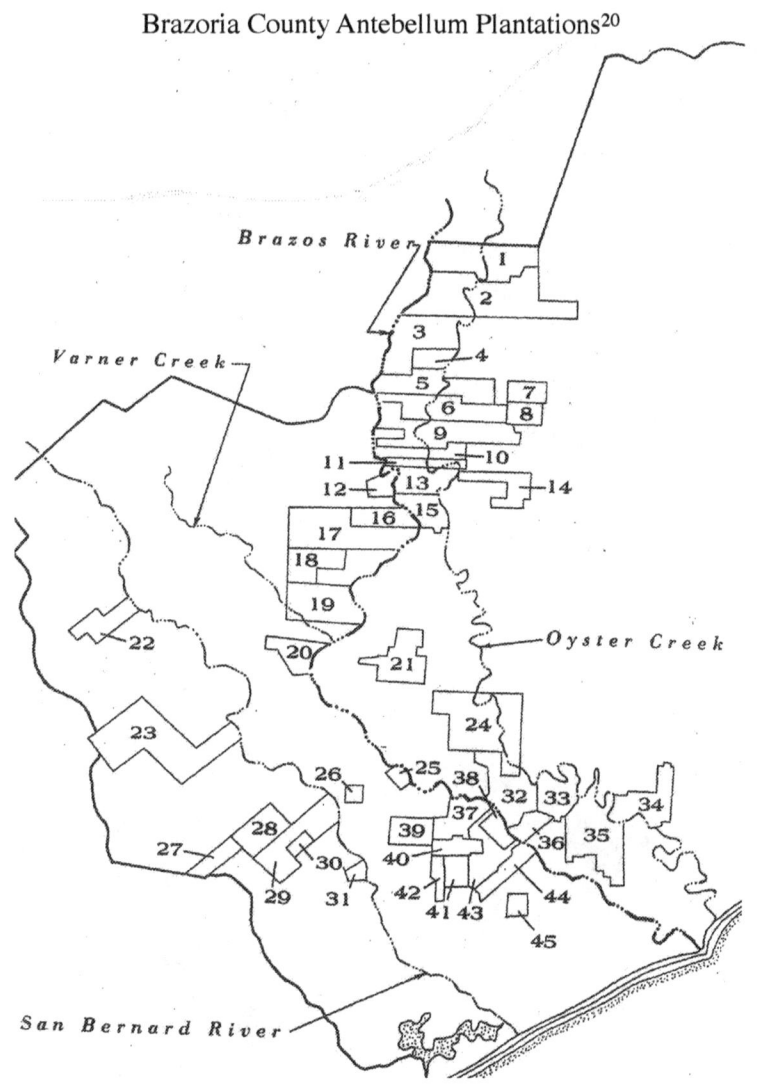

---

[20] Ibid

II.
"STRIKE!"
The Production of Granulated Sugar In Antebellum Texas

By virtue of their geographic location to rivers and the Gulf of Mexico, their long growing season, and their sugar cane productive soils, Brazoria, Fort Bend, Wharton and Matagorda Counties became known, in the 1840s, as the "Sugar Bowl" of Texas. Sugar became an even more important crop after an infestation of cotton worms severely cut cotton production in the area. Local farmers and planters became dependent on both sugar cane and cotton.[1]

William R. Johnson, in his 1961 history of the sugar industry in Texas stated, "Although the sugar industry was fast expanding in the early 1840s, it was still in an experimental stage. Sugar mills used horses or mules for powering their cane crushers and most used wooden rollers for crushing the cane."[2] In 1843, Captain William Duncan erected a steam mill on his Caney Creek plantation; the first steam powered mill in Texas. Duncan must have switched from the cultivation of the Creole variety of sugar cane to the purple ribbon variety that had a greater yield of juice. Due to its very tough fiber, purple ribbon required the stronger power of steam and metal rollers for crushing its cane.[3] The variety of purple ribbon cane spread rapidly. By 1844, there were 29 sugar mills in Brazoria County.[4]

In the 1840s, a substantial amount of money was required to establish a sugar plantation and mill. An 1843 estimate for land, equipment and slaves was $39,000 per planter.[5] In 1845,

---

[1] Johnson, William R. 1961 *A Short History of The Sugar Industry in Texas*, Texas Gulf Coast Historical Association Publications, Vol. 5, #1 April 1961, Page 13
[2] Ibid, Page 14
[3] Ibid, Page 13
[4] Creighton, James A., *A Narrative History of Brazoria County,* Brazoria County Historical Commission, Texian Press, Waco, 1975, Page 197
[5] Ibid

Eli Mercer in Wharton County refined 50,000 pounds of sugar and raised enough crops to feed and clothe his slaves. Each of his slaves earned him a profit of $500 in sugar.[6] In 1846 a cost estimate for building a sugar mill and acquiring the approximately 50 slaves needed (at $500 per slave) was about $50,000.[7] Planters had learned that in the "Sugar Bowl" a single hand could cultivate about four acres of sugar cane plus enough corn and vegetables to support himself.[8]

$50,000 was a very large sum of money in the pre Civil War years; however, farmers in Texas were far better off than their counterparts in the other Southern states during this period. Statistical studies done on public and economic records by Richard G. Lowe and Randolph B. Campbell show that Texans increased in wealth and property at a much higher rate than farmers and planters in other Southern states. Their study shows that between 1850 and 1860, over 75% of the Texas population was involved in farming and that slave owners operated 33% of those farms. More farmers in Texas owned their land than in any of the other Southern states.[9]

Most farmers in Texas, the non-slave owners, increased the value of their real property by more than 50% in the 1850s. The slave owners doubled the value of their real estate and increased the size of their slave forces. The slave owning minority in Texas controlled two thirds of the agricultural property in the state, and produced nine-tenths of all the cotton. This is a higher percentage than all other cotton producing states. Farming in Texas grew rapidly between 1850 and 1860. Land and slaves were cheaper than in other Southern states.[10] At the beginning of the Civil War, there were thousands of untilled agricultural acres available in Texas.

---

[6] Johnson, 1961, Page 16
[7] Ibid, Page 15
[8] Ibid, Page 13
[9] Lowe, R.G. and R.B. Campbell, 1987 *Planters and Plain Folk: Agriculture in Antebellum Texas.* Southern Methodist University Press, Dallas   Pages 181-190
[10] Ibid

Between the 1820s and 1860 the slave population in Texas increased. There were 1316 slaves listed in the 1840 census of Brazoria County. In 1847, 3013 slaves were listed; 64.92% of the total population. By 1860, 5110 slaves represented 71.41% of the population.

The slave census in Brazoria County in 1860, lists 158 slave owners owning between 1 - 19 slaves and 67 planters owning between 20 and 343 slaves. A slave owner was considered a planter when they owned 20 or more slaves. Many farmers and sons of planters called themselves "planters" because this status implied that they no longer worked in the fields side by side with their slaves as was the case with many small slave owners.

Many planters grew both cotton and sugar in the Brazos River valley area; each crop was insurance for the failure of the other. The intensive labor required throughout the year for both crops required a large labor force.

Cotton was very labor intensive. Cotton fields were prepared in January and February, and the cotton was planted in March. These plants had to be hoed and tended until harvest time. Cotton would start blossoming in May. In June the cotton gin was made ready for the harvest, and the storage buildings prepared. Baskets were made to carry the cotton boles. Because of the time consuming tasks of picking, ginning and baling cotton, the cotton was sometimes picked when the boles opened and then stored. Ginning and baling of cotton could continue through the fall, winter, and early spring until the entire crop was processed. Between 1850 and 1860 about three million bales of cotton were produced in Brazoria County and averaged about 11.61 cents per pound.[11]

The planting of sugar cane began in January and February. The fields required extensive drainage canals and ditches to prevent standing water in the fields, which caused the roots to rot.

---

[11] Creighton, 1975 Page 217

Keeping the fields well drained was a year-round job because sugar cane in Texas "ratoons." This means that it will grow more than one crop from a single planting,[12] sometimes producing for three or more years. Sugar cane, when planted, was placed in a high ridge with ridges about six feet apart. Planters had a wide variety of methods for placing the seed cane in the rows. Placed lengthwise in the ridge, the cane was cut separating the "joints" or "eyes" and then covered with dirt. The cane ridges were carefully hoed and tended for about three months until the cane was high enough to prevent weeds from growing in the cane fields. During the summer months, the preparations for harvest were intense. The sugar mill had to be cleaned and repaired. Hogsheads and barrels had to be built. Granulated sugar was stored and shipped in hogsheads and the ungranulated sugar, molasses, was stored and shipped in barrels.

A hogshead is a large barrel or cask: in the United States, a hogshead contains about 63 gallons of liquid measurement or 2.86 Hectoliters of dry measurement.[13] In Great Britain, a hogshead contains from 50 to 100 gallons. A statute of Richard III in 1483 fixed a hogshead of wine at 63 wine -gallons, i.e., 52 1/2 imperial gallons.[14]

For each hogshead of sugar produced, three to five cords of wood were needed for fuel in the sugar mill.[15] The Peach Point Farm Journal (Perry plantation) of 1859 states that over 950 cords of wood were cut that year for the mill.[16] About the middle of October the cutting of the cane and the processing of sugar started. About 1300 pounds of raw sugar cane would yield one hogshead of sugar and two to three barrels of molasses.[17] Most planters kept their mills going 24

---

[12] Johnson, 1961 Page 15
[13] Dick, William B., *Encyclopedia of Practical Receipts and Processes*, Dick and Fitzgerald, 1890
[14] Encyclopedia Britannic, 1949
[15] Creighton, 1975 Page 200
[16] Platter, Allen Andrew, *Educational, Social, and Economic characteristics of the Plantation Culture of Brazoria County*, 1961, PhD Dissertation, University of Houston Page 52
[17] Creighton, 1975 Page 201

hours a day until all the sugar cane was processed. James A. Creighton, in his 1975 history of Brazoria County calculated that the "Average production for a twenty-four hour period was from eight to ten hogsheads." [18]

There were three reasons the field hands had to harvest the cane quickly. The juice in the cane began to lose its sugar content, sucrose, as soon as it was cut. The juice needed to be boiled down into sugar within twenty four hours to have maximum sugar content. Since the mills operated on a twenty-four hour schedule, enough cane had to be cut each day to keep the mill busy during the night. If cane was still standing in the fields when the first hard frost occurred, that cane would be lost.

Field hands went into the cane fields dressed in armor. They padded their legs, ankles, and feet to protect themselves from their own machetes and cane knives. With gloved hands, they attacked the cane almost like cutting corn. The leaves were stripped from the cane, the unripe joints were cut, and then they severed the stalk from its roots and threw it on the ground. Other field hands picked up the stalks and carried them to wagons for transportation to the mill.[19] On some plantations metal tracks with carts ran from the field to the mill for easy transport. The levees for the tracks are still visible at Osceola Plantation in Brazoria County.

When the cane reached the mill, it was placed on a conveyor belt powered by horses or mules and transported to the second floor of the mill to the cane crushers, which were powered by steam engines. Early cane crushers were of wood and powered by horses or mules. As the cane passed through the three rollers, two below and one above, the cane was "squeezed" and the cane juice extracted. The juice fell into a vat below the rollers. At the Lake Jackson plantation,

---

[18] Creighton, 1975 Page 200
[19] Johnson, 1961 Page 13

the receiving vat had a copper sieve cover that allowed the juice to enter the vat, but prohibited any plant particles from getting into the liquid.

From the vat below the rollers, the juice went by pipe to clarification vats on the first floor. The crushed cane fibers, called bagasse, went from the rollers down a trough, which usually led outside the building. When dried, it could be used as fuel, cattle feed, and to repair the levees.[20]

The clarification vats were usually lined with copper or lead. In these large vats the juice was strained, by various methods, to remove the larger impurities. From these first vats, the juice passed into a series of open kettles for clarification and evaporation.[21]

A "train of kettles" or "set of kettles" was usually four to six large iron kettles arranged in a

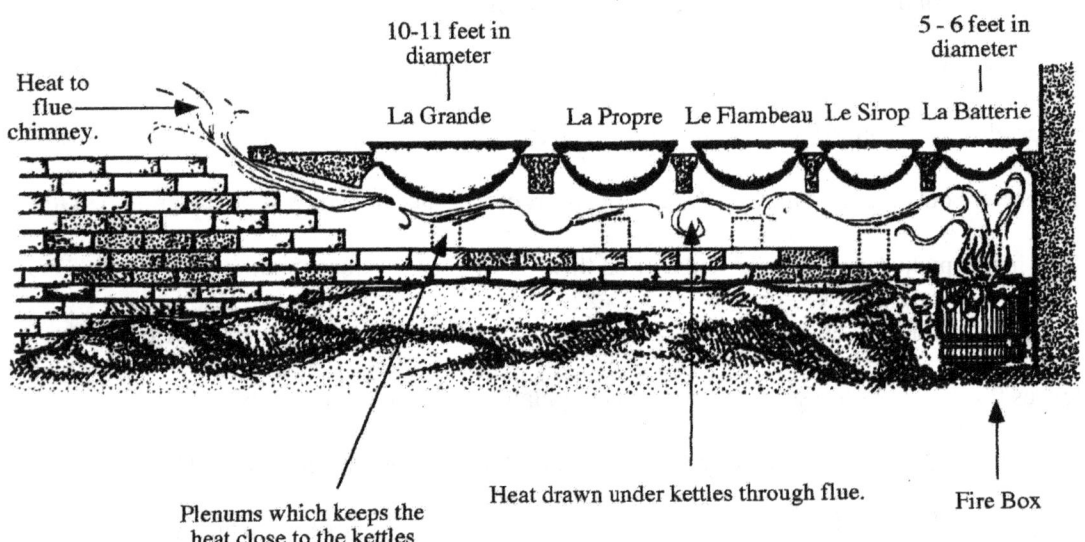

Train of Sugar Evaporation Kettles[22]

---

[20] Sitterson, J.C. 1953 *Sugar Country: The Cane Sugar Industry in the South, 1753-1950* University of Kentucky Press
[21] Johnson, 1961
[22] Geerlings, 1912 *The World's Cane Sugar Industry*, London, Norman Rogers, Scanned and altered from Figure 9, Page 106, Preservation Plan and Program for Verner-Hogg Plantation State Historical Park, Texas Parks and Wildlife Department.

line and set in solid masonry. The heat used in the reduction (evaporation) process came from a fire under the smallest kettle, the *batterie,* and was pulled under and around the kettles by the draw of a tall chimney near the largest kettle, the *grande*. Louisiana sugar makers referred to the various kettles by names: *la grande, la propre, le flambeau, le sirop,* and *la batterie*. There were sometime two *grandes,* to expedite the first part of the process. The reduction (evaporation) kettles could range in size from 5 to 11 feet in diameter for the largest kettles to 3 to 6 feet in diameter for the smallest.[23] The *la grande* kettle on display at the Brazoria County Historical Museum in Angleton, Texas, is 7'4" in diameter, 24" deep and holds 576 gallons.

The first kettle was filled with juice flowing from the reservoir vats. A mixture of cane juice and slaked lime ("...6 to 24 cubic inches of slaked lime to two or three gallons of juice, forming a milk."[24]) was added as a clarifying agent, as the juice was poured into the *grande*. As the juice began to boil a greenish-gray scum formed on the surface and became thicker as the temperature rose. As soon as a watery vapor forced itself up through the scum, skimming began and the scum was removed. When the skimming was completed the juice was ladled into the next kettle, where scum not removed in the *grande* was boiled up and removed. This boiling and skimming process continued until the juice passed through all the kettles. Above the kettles, a steam chimney carried away vapor from the rapidly evaporating cane juice.

The last and smallest kettle, the *batterie,* received the most concentrated juice. When the juice reached the evaporation point when granulation could begin, "strike" was called out by the sugar maker. "Strike" meant to strike it from the heat; to remove it from the *batterie*. The juice was ladled into cooling troughs, where it granulated into crystals.[25]

---

[23] Sitterson, 1953 Page 135, and Geerlings, 1912
[24] Geerlings, 1912
[25] Johnson, 1961 Page 25

These cooling trays, coolers, were oblong wooden troughs, made of two-inch pinewood that were usually ten feet long, five feet wide, and ten to twelve inches deep. They were set parallel to the train in a double row, six in each row. Each cooler held three "strikes." The three strikes were not added one on top of the other, but each was cooled in a separate cooler and then poured together into a single cooler. While the sugar was cooling, the sugar master would take a light wooden instrument, like a small rake without teeth, and move it up and down the cooler to agitate the mass and promote crystallization.[26] The cooling trays held from one to one and a half hogsheads of sugar; 1,000 to 1500 pounds. It took from six to fourteen hours for granulation to be completed.[27]

When the granulation was complete, slaves would get into the cooling trays wearing only a "breech clout" and with shovels, they would shovel out the sugar and the molasses, the uncrystallized juice. They shoveled the mixture into copper basins or tubs carried on the heads of slave women who carried them to the purging house and emptied the contents into a hogshead barrel until each hogshead was full.[28]

The hogsheads rested on timbers above a molasses barrel or cistern. The molasses drained into the molasses barrel through a hole in the bottom of the hogshead. Twenty to thirty days were required for the molasses to drain from the hogshead. When the molasses had completely drained, then the hogsheads and the molasses barrels were ready for shipment to market in New Orleans.[29] Approximately three barrels of molasses were drained from each hogshead of sugar.[30]

---

[26] Olcott, 1857 Page 97
[27] Johnson, 1961 Page 25
[28] Olcott, 1857 Page 97
[29] Johnson, 1961 Page 25
[30] Creighton, 1975 Page 201

The two most difficult parts of the sugar making process were the adding of lime and knowing just when to call the "strike." Litmus paper, when touched to the fresh cut sugar cane, would turn red if the juice was acidic. If the juice showed acidity, then soda, or soda ash [$NaCO_3$] could be added until the juice was neutral. If the juice did not show acidity, then lime [CaO] was added.[31] If the proper amount of lime was added in the *grande*, then the juice when transferred to the *flambeau*, would be a pale yellowish wine color. If too much lime had been added, the juice would have an alkaline smell and a reddish color. If not enough lime was added; the juice would not boil freely. How much lime used depended on the ripeness of the cane; the riper the cane the smaller amount of lime was needed. The amount of lime increased with the greenness of the cane.[32]

Determining when to "strike," was also a balance of many variables. Sitterson in his 1953 history of sugar gave this explanation.

> To ascertain when the syrup had attained the proper consistency for granulation or for being struck, it was common practice to thrust a large copper spoon with wooden handle into the *battery*. If when the spoon was withdrawn, the syrup had a grained appearance and was so thick that it covered the spoon in a film and drained from it slowly, it had been cooked sufficiently. It was then discharged by the bucket into an adjoining reservoir, from which it flowed to the coolers for granulation. Another method of determining the striking point was to place a little syrup on the thumb and draw it out into a thread with a forefinger. If the thread broke dry and rose in a spiral form, the boiling was good. The time required to bring a charge from the *grande* to the crystallizing point varied from one to two hours, depending on the richness of the juice and the setting of the kettles.[33]

---

[31] *The Planter*, February 7, 1845 Columbia, Texas, from "Southern Calendar for December"
[32] Sitterson, 1953 Page 143
[33] Ibid

Another method for determining the point of "strike" was to use a thermometer in the smallest kettle and remove the syrup to the cooling trays when the temperature reached 239 degrees Fahrenheit.[34]

The cleanliness of the mill was another important factor in the process. Every part and every vessel through which the sugar liquid passed had to be kept clean. If impurities lodged within the joints or crevices, it could become putrid and infect the pure juice coming in contact with it. It was recommended in an article to planters in the *The Planters Gazette* that the "cylinders, mill bed, and channels, should be well sprinkled with lime when ever the work is stopped..."[35]

Sugar cane production in Texas was not consistent from year to year.

Sugar Production 1852-1858[36]

	1852	1853	1854	1855	1856	1857	1858
Sugar Bowl	11,023	8,228	7,513	8,977	150	2,000	6,000
Brazoria County	7,357	5,239	5,681	6,633	0	0	5,150

Sugar Bowl = Brazoria, Fort Bend, Wharton and Matagorda Counties

Natural disasters, such as too much rain, caused root rot; freezes killed the crops; droughts prohibited the proper amount of juice to form; and hurricanes blew the cane to the ground wiping out a crop. A "severe drought in 1850 stunted the sugar cane and caused only the lower three or

---

[34] *The Planters Gazette* December 31, 1842 Vol. 1 #7, Columbia, Texas
[35] Ibid
[36] Creighton, 1975 Page 205

four feet of stalk to ripen."[37] 1852 was the best sugar crop in Texas with 11,023 hogsheads produced, valued at $40 per hogshead.[38] P.A. Champomier, a Louisiana sugar authority, published yearly reports on the Louisiana sugar crop and after 1852, he began to include Texas yields.[39] The 1853 crop did not equal the 1852 crop. Sugar production in 1854 was lower than 1852 due to a wet spring, a drought in the summer and a hurricane in the fall.[40] There was almost no sugar produced in 1856 because the winter of 1855-56 was so severe that most of the seed cane was killed.[41] In 1857 five months of drought in the spring and summer months limited production to 2,000 hogsheads.[42] 1858 can be described as an "average" yield. During poor sugar years, planters had cotton as their cash crop.

The larger mills in the "Sugar Bowl" were constructed of brick and were two stories high. Their tall chimneys, one for the boiler, one for the flue, and one for venting the kettles, gave them a castle like appearance. At one end of the mill were the steam engine, the cane crushers and the clarification vats. Next came the "train of kettles" to reduce the sugar juice down to granulated sugar. At the far end, away from the boilers and fires, was the purgery where the crystallization took place in the cooling trays and when cooled, the sugar was placed in the hogsheads. Under the hogsheads were placed the barrels to collect the molasses, the uncrystallized syrup that drained by gravity from the hogsheads. Beyond the purgery was the storeroom where hogsheads and barrels were stored for shipment.[43] The purgeries were kept as

---

[37] Johnson, 1961 Page 26
[38] Ibid, Page 28
[39] Ibid, Page 26, P.A. Champomier, *Statement of the Sugar Crop Made in Louisiana in 1852-1858*, Cook, Young and Co., New Orleans
[40] Ibid, Page 32
[41] Ibid, Page 34
[42] Ibid, Page 36
[43] Creighton, 1975 Page 199

warm as possible to enhance the draining of the syrup. Some plantations used stoves to keep the temperature around 80 degrees.[44]

Crieghton has given us this verbal description of the mills in Texas. In Chapter 8, we will discuss what we have learned about the mills through archaeological excavation. Sugar production by planters in Texas between 1852 and 1858 is listed in the Appendices.

http://web.mac.com/joan_few

---

[44] Sitterson, 1953 Page 143

III.

The Abner and Margaret Jackson Family,

Brazoria County, Texas

Margaret Inabinet was born about 1807, the daughter of Baltis Inabinet Sr. and Mary Moorer.[1] In 1830, Margaret married John Strobel in Colleton County, South Carolina. John was born in 1803 in Dorchester County, South Carolina, and was the son of Albert Strobel, and the grandson of Johannes Casper Strobel.[2] Margaret and John had a son, Lewis[3] Martin Strobel, born on September 16, 1831 in Colleton County, South Carolina.[4] John Strobel died in the early 1830s leaving Margaret a widow with land and slaves. She married Abner Jackson about 1834. Abner Jackson was born in Virginia around 1809. Abner and Margaret had three children in South Carolina: Arsenath[5] (1835), John C. (1838), and Andrew J. (1840). A fourth child, George W., was born in Georgia (1842), and their youngest child, Abner Jr. was born in Texas (1847).[6]

In 1838, Abner Jackson lived on the Trinity River and harvested one crop.[7] During this time period, people migrating to Texas may have numbered 7,000 a year. During a six month

---

[1] Personal correspondence with Pat Cashon Johnson, descendant of Margaret Strobel Jackson. Baltis Inabinet Sr. was born in 1747.
[2] Ibid
[3] Spelled Louis in some records.
[4] Personal correspondence with Pat Johnson, also LDS Records, Film #453986, Page Number 59, Reference Number, 60223.
[5] The spelling, Arsenath, will be used in this book because it is the spelling used by her cousin, Abner Strobel, in his narratives and was the way her name was signed by her brother, George, on legal documents. Acenath, Asenath, Asinith, Arceneth, Arsnith are other ways the name is spelled in various records.
[6] Brazoria County Census of 1850
[7] Strobel, Abner J. 1926, The Old Plantations and Their Owners of Brazoria County, Texas, Published by Union National Bank, Houston, Texas, Reprinted in 1980 under, "Historical Scrapbook of West Columbia, Texas, Page 42

period in 1838, "fifty-nine ships made 101 trips between Texas ports and New Orleans."[8] The 1840 Census lists an A. Jackson living in Liberty County, Texas, with 1825 acres under survey and 11 horses. Jackson removed his slaves from Georgia in 1842.[9] The 1842 Tax Assessor Rolls for Brazoria County list Jackson with 74 slaves and 4 horses.[10] By 1843, Jackson was developing Retrieve, his first cotton and cane plantation. Jackson contracted with John Mady to build "running gear for gin and outside cotton preparations."[11] Tax records for 1843, lists Jackson with 84 slaves, 8 horses, and 248 head of cattle.[12] In 1844, Jackson purchased with heavy mortgages, 2892 acres of land on Oyster Creek, four miles north of the present city of Lake Jackson, from Emily Perry and William and Elizabeth Hill.[13]

Margaret and Abner Jackson probate records imply that Retrieve was partially established with Margaret Strobel Jackson's money and slaves. Tax rolls indicate that Jackson also purchased in 1844, an additional 1000 acres of land in Harris County[14] as well as 1600 acres (approximately) that were added to the Retrieve plantation from the William H. Wharton Estate.[15] It was from this initial development of Retrieve Plantation that Abner Jackson built the Jackson fortune.

Abner Jackson Strobel, born on September 6, 1858 in Brazoria County, was the son of Lewis and Elizabeth Washington Strobel[16] and the grandson of Margaret Strobel Jackson. He

---

[8] Creighton, James A., "A Narrative History of Brazoria County," Brazoria County Historical Commission, Printed by Texian Press, Waco, 1975, Page 156
[9] Brazoria County Deed: 1844, D-347
[10] Historical Resource Survey of the Lake Jackson Plantation (Survey Report 89-01) July 24, 1989, Gross, W.S.; Pollan J.T. Jr.; Smith, J.L.; Wayland, J.S. Wayland D.J., Page 4
[11] Brazoria County Deed: 1843, B-319, Ibid Page 4
[12] Survey Report 89-01, Page 4
[13] Brazoria County Deed: 1844, Vol. B-403, 411, Survey Report 89-01, Page 4
[14] Survey Report 89-01, Page 4
[15] Brazoria County Deed: 1844, Vol. D: 14,16,18, Survey Report 89-01, Page 4
[16] LDS IGI Record, Film Number: 453986, Page 12, Reference # 60227

described the Retrieve Plantation in his narratives as one of the finest plantations in the county. It contained a two story brick residence, brick cabins, a large brick sugar house with double-set of kettles, and a large brick oven to cook for the slaves.[17] One half interest in Retrieve was conveyed to Henry R.W. Hill of New Orleans who accepted it under covenant with Thomas L. Hamilton. Hamilton was the trustee for Mrs. Elizabeth Hamilton of South Carolina, who was the wife of James Hamilton.[18] Abner Jackson and James Hamilton were business partners before Jackson came to Texas.

Abner J. Strobel in his narrative history of Brazoria Country printed in 1926, gave this description of James Hamilton.

> Gen. James Hamilton was of an old Huguenot South Carolina family. On the appointment of General Rusk as Secretary of War, and the command of the army falling upon General Felix Huston, a joint resolution of the Congress of Texas invited General Hamilton to become a Texan and commander-in-chief of the army. He became a Texan, but declined the honor of commanding the army. Hamilton had been a gallant soldier in the war of 1812-15, had been Governor of South Carolina and United States Senator from that state. In the Senate of South Carolina early in 1836, when George McDuffie, to the regret of his friends throughout the Union, had denounced the Texas revolution in terms showing his ignorance of the issues involved, General Hamilton introduced counter resolutions and by one of the most eloquent speeches ever delivered in America, carried them almost unanimously. General Hamilton performed distinguished services for Texas. He was appointed Commissioner to England, France, Holland and Belgium to secure a loan of five million dollars. In this he was unsuccessful, but on his return to Europe, he secured the acknowledgment of Texas Independence by Great Britain, France and Belgium .... The General started for South Carolina, I believe, in 1857, and while off the coast of Florida his vessel was wrecked and sunk by one of those terrible hurricanes. When all had put on their life belts, there was one lady on board who had none. General Hamilton immediately gave her his and went down with the ship.[19]

---

[17] Strobel, Page 45
[18] Brazoria County Deed: 1844, B-481, Survey Report 89-01, Page 4
[19] Strobel, Page 45

In 1845, Jackson, James Hamilton, James Perry, and William G. Hill organized the Brazos Canal Company,[20] to transport goods to Galveston Bay by bypassing the mouth of the Brazos with its treacherous sand bars. "Jackson had to transport any produce overland several miles from his plantation headquarters located on the bank of Oyster Creek east to a steamboat landing on Bastrop Bayou. From this location a small boat could travel down Bastrop Bayou to Bastrop Bay (San Luis Bay) and then to Galveston Bay. The opening of a canal between Oyster Creek and Bastrop Bayou would open the way for shipping directly from his plantation."[21] Though the company was not completely successful in all their goals, they did complete a canal between Oyster Creek and Bastrop Bayou; noted in a field survey by Thomas Borden in 1848.[22]

Also during 1845, Jackson purchased 405 acres for $1,822 from John A. Murle. This tract would be part of the Jackson Plantation, the "Lake Place," located south of Retrieve. Abner Jackson had been able to build Retrieve by using heavy mortgages on the property. Jackson was financially overextended with mortgages and loans.

In 1846, Jackson attempted to borrow more money from James Reed. Mr. Reed wrote to Mr. James Perry, explaining his refusal to take Jackson's note, "...for the very reason that he has no intention whatever of paying until he is forced by law to do so, independent of this he boast of the privilege the law gives him. He has made two good crops since I took his note and he has not shown any willingness to appropriate one dollar of the proceeds towards this debt but said to Mr. Butler that the law might take its course."[23] (Letter in Appendices)

---

[20] Brazoria County Deed: 1845, B-36
[21] Unpublished Document by James L. Smith: "Transportation Enterprises for the Brazos River Valley, 1836-1861" by the Brazosport Archaeological Society
[22] Platter, Page 92, Brazoria County Deed: 1845, N-538
[23] James A. Perry papers, Brazoria County Historical Museum Library, Angleton, Texas
Courtesy of James L. Smith

In 1847, James and Emily Perry sued Jackson for back payment of debts and won the case.[24] This caused a sudden reversal of fortunes for Jackson. Jackson owed five mortgages at this time totaling $15,957.66.[25] He was also in arrears of over $40,000 to the estate of John Ferguson. Three letters, contained in the Appendices, from James Hamilton to James Perry document Hamilton's involvement in the Oyster Creek debt.

"Abner Jackson's partner, Henry R.W. Hill, became aware of the critical financial situation and assumed title to Retrieve Plantation. He issued a mortgage to Burl McBride, administrator of the estate of John Ferguson of South Carolina, for $30,000. He also bought out Jackson's interest by securing two notes totaling $9,200 owed Jackson by James Hamilton. Hill then appointed James Hamilton to manage the Retrieve Plantation.[26] Hill further conveyed Power of Attorney to Thomas Hamilton.[27] Jackson then paid off the mortgages owed by him against Retrieve."[28]

Jackson still owned the 405 acres south of Retrieve. In a letter, dated April 1849, to Samuel May Williams of Galveston, Jackson stated that he had 200 acres of cane planted and was bargaining for a sugar mill.[29] With luck in his favor, Jackson mortgaged the 600 acres where he was living, which he did not own, and the 405 acres he owned, to Robert and David G. Mills for $3,625.[30] Robert and David G. Mills owned the Lowwood and Bynum sugar plantations and the Palo Alto cotton plantation. They were also Galveston merchants and bankers.

---

[24] Brazoria County DCM: 1847, 755/756
[25] Brazoria County Deed: 1848,E-52
[26] Brazoria County Deed: 1848, E-48, Survey Report 89-01, Page 6
[27] Brazoria County Deed: 1848, E - 174, Survey Report 89-01, Page 6
[28] Brazoria County Deed: 1848,: 53-55, Survery Report 89-01, Page 6
[29] S.M. Williams Papers, Rosenberg Library, Galveston, Texas
[30] Brazoria County Deed 1849, E-244, Survey Report 89-01, Page 6

A month later, Jackson mortgaged the same property that he had mortgaged to the Mills brothers to Nathan Jarvis of New Orleans for $3,202.[31] In these two deeds, the term "Lake Jackson," plantation is used for the first time.

Jackson finally purchased the 600 acre property, that he had mortgaged to the Mills brothers and to Nathan Jarvis, from LeRoy M. Wiley of New York City for $3,000.[32]

Abner J. Strobel gives this description of the Lake Jackson Plantation is his narrative of the old plantations.

> Major Jackson ... opened up the Lake Jackson Plantation during the period 1842 to 1845. His first home was made of logs from the nearby forest, mostly elm and ash. He soon, however, converted every building, cabins, sugar house and residence, into brick made on the plantation, and stuccoed with cement fully an inch thick, which made all buildings look like they were made from solid rock. The residence was a twelve room two-story house in the shape of an "I," with six galleries, and immense brick pillars the entire length of the galleries. It was cool in summer and warm in winter with its large fire places. Built Colonial style, the residence cost, exclusive of slave labor, over twenty-five thousand dollars completed. The lake abounded in fish.... There were boats in plenty for the use of the guests and family, and the lake abounded in ducks in winter, and at that time and as late as 1868, plenty of deer, bears and turkeys could be found. The sugar house was built of brick, and the best of machinery for the making of sugar was obtained. There was an artificial island made in the lake, said to have cost $10,000 and is visible to this day [1926]. Fine orchards and gardens were on the plantation. Peaches, pears, quince, plums grapes and strawberries were raised. Brick walks were laid in the orchard and garden. The slaves had use of both orchards and gardens.[33]

---

[31] Brazoria County Deed 1849, E-247, Survey Report 89-01, Page 6
[32] Brazoria County Deed: 1849, E-297, Survey Report 89-01, Page 6
[33] Strobel, Page 42

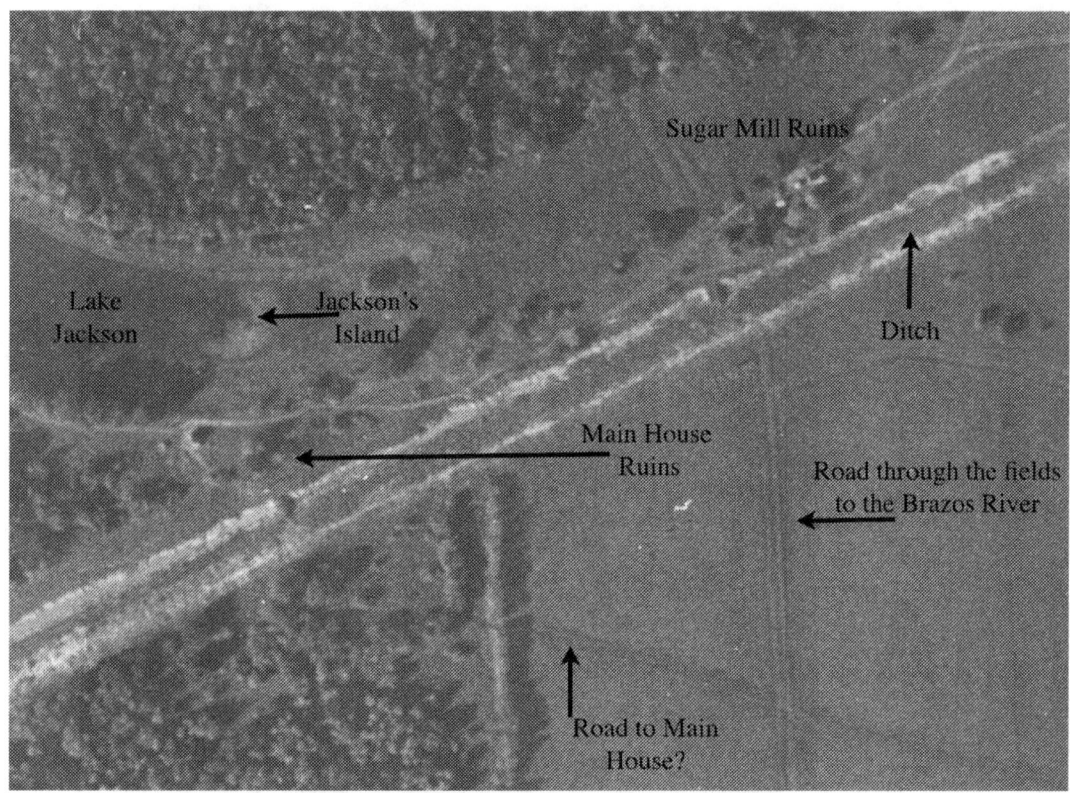

Aerial Photo Taken in the 1930s or 1940s
Used by permission of The Brazosport Archaeological Society

In 1850, 1200 acres adjoining the plantation on the south side were mortgaged from M.J. and W.B. Victor of Kentucky for $3000. Later that year, Jackson acquired 326 and 7/8 acres from the Victors, making his property reach all the way to the Brazos River.[34] "The Lake Jackson Plantation main house was built in 1851 on the south shore of Lake Jackson on the 1200 acres acquired from the Victors."[35] According to the 1850 Brazoria County Census taken on October 14 at the Jackson Plantation Abner Jackson was age 40; Margaret Jackson was 43; Arsenath M. was 15; John C. was 12 and at school in Brazoria County; Andrew was 10; George W. was 8; and Abner Jr. was 3.

---

[34] Brazoria County Deed 1850, Vol. F: 345,533, Survey Report 89-01, Page 6
[35] Survey Report 89-01, Page 6

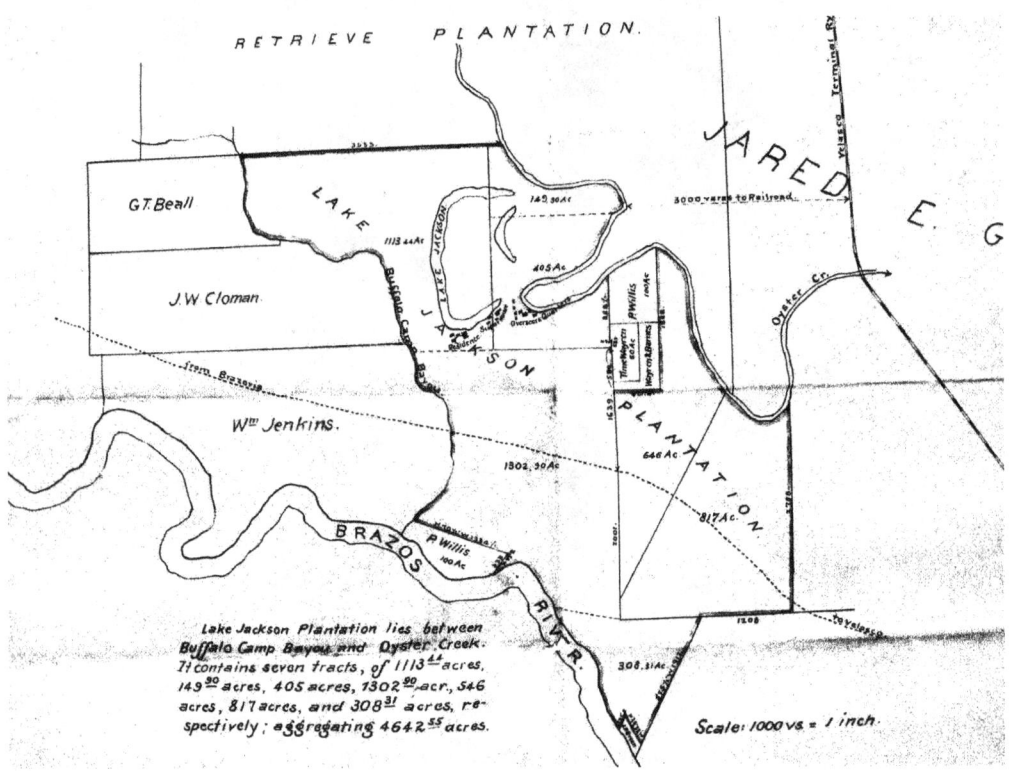

This map shows the 7 tracts of Lake Jackson Plantation totaling 4642.55 acres.

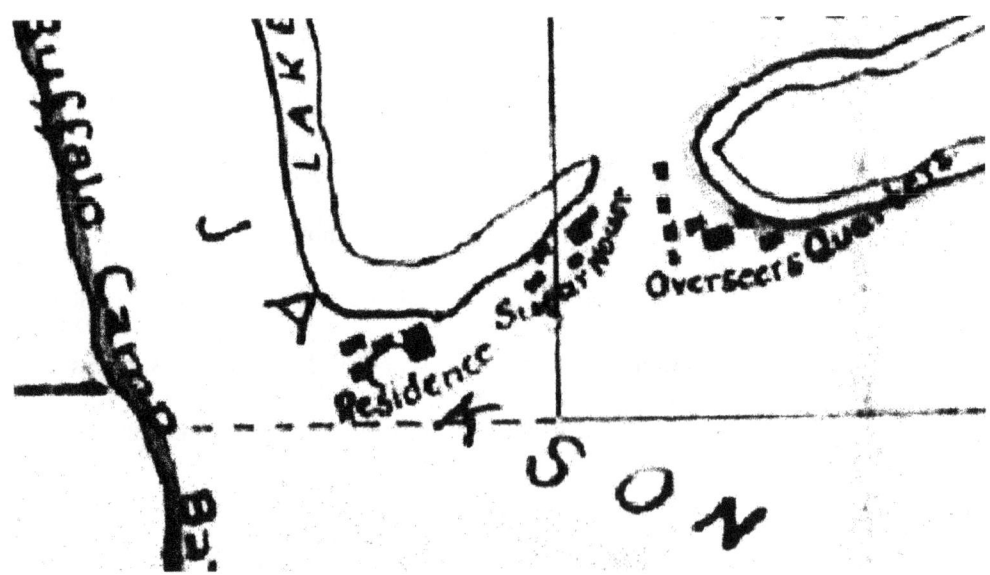

Enlargement of Building Area

A map recently acquired by the Lake Jackson Historical Association shows the extent of the plantation; map copy courtesy of Johnney Pollan.

An enlargement of the map on the facing page shows the Plantation House area, the Sugar House and surrounding buildings, and the Overseers Quarters. The structures around the Overseer's house may represent the slave quarters. (Map enlargement courtesy of Johnney Pollan.)

In 1852, Jackson produced 295 hogsheads of sugar with horse driven machinery and with James Hamilton at Retrieve an additional 450 hogsheads. Retrieve had a double train of kettles and a steam engine that enhanced its production capabilities over the Jackson plantation.

Though sugar production at Lake Jackson Plantation fell off for the next few years, sugar production remained a steady cash crop for Jackson. During 1853, 1854, and 1855, production was better at Retrieve Plantation than at Lake Jackson.

At this time (1854), Burl McBride held the mortgage on the Retrieve Plantation and filed a civil suit against James Hamilton and Henry R.W. Hill.[36] McBride won the case and on February 6, 1855, the Retrieve Plantation was auctioned by the sheriff to Henry D. Lesesne for $31,715.75.[37] The following October, Lesesne offered the property for sale.

In the October 23, 1855, edition of the local newspaper, the Democrat and Planter, this advertisement appeared.

> VALUABLE SUGAR ESTATE IN TEXAS FOR SALE
>
> All that PLANTATION called the RETRIEVE, situated on Oyster Creek in the County of Brazoria, Texas, containing 3275 acres, more or less, and bounding on lands now or lately of Asa Mitchell, M. Wiley, and S.F. Austin. About 1000 acres are in cultivation, of which 500 acres are well

---

[36] Survey Report 89-01, Page 6
[37] Brazoria County Deed: 1855, G-182

stocked with sugar cane. On the premises are a sugar house, steam engine, mill and kettles, a dwelling house, and kitchen of brick, and negro cabins. The property is under lease, for the current year, and is to be delivered up at the end of the year in good condition for making a sugar crop next season. Possession to be delivered to the purchaser accordingly.

Terms - One third cash; residue [sic] in one, two, three, and four years in equal payments, bearing interest from time of sale, and secured by mortgage of the property; the buildings to be insured and the policy assigned as a further security.

Persons disposed to purchase, may treat with his Excellency, E.M. Pease, Governor of Texas, who is prepared to give full information as to the condition and value of the property, or with the subscriber.

October 16th, Henry D. Lesesne, Charleston, S.C

Abner Jackson wrote to Governor Pease and received a reply. In his response to the Governor on January 9, 1856, he implies that he has been leasing the Retrieve Plantation and raising cane using his slaves.

Jany 9th 1856
Gov. E M Pease
    Austin
        Dear Sir,

I red [sic] your esteemed favor of 26th last informing me that you had mislaid a letter from me in reference to the sale or purchase of the Retrieve Plantation etc. In that letter I proposed to purchase the property on the following terms at the price of the McBride debt and on the terms set forth in Mr. Lesesnes advertisement.

Now to be more explicit I propose to purchase the property and pay the McBride debt reserving the amount to myself that may be collected from the trust Estate or I will pay you Rent for the next year (commencing at the time of the expiration of my present Lease and same conditions that I have it for the present). I will give Thirty five (3500) Hundred Dollars as rent. I will be done making sugar in about 8 or ten days and if I am not to occupy it for this year I will be under the necessity of taking the Hands to another place, and in that event this place would (if not cultivated) depreciate very much the cane would be Lost etc. I wrote to Mr. Lesesne at the time that I wrote to you and have not had a word from him. I fear that my Letter has miscarried and it is now too Late to write to him. As soon as I am done I will be compelled to draw off my hands unless I can hear from you or Mr. Lesesne. I wish you to be certain to write by return mail.

With kinds regds I remn very truly yrs

A. Jackson

In 1856, Jackson purchased Retrieve from Lesesne for $46,042 and mortgaged one-half interest to Elizabeth Hamilton.[38] On October 13th, 1856, Jackson borrowed $6,343.84 from Lesesne.

During these years of plantation acquisition, Margaret and Abner did not ignore the educational needs of their children. "Maj. Abner Jackson sent two sons to Norwich University, Vermont, and kept them there four years until they finished; [then sent] one to Kentucky and one to Georgia... He said the reason he sent his sons to different colleges was that if all were sent to one college, they would want to run the college. Besides, he said, it would give them different views and ideas of life, by being sent to different localities."[39] In 1861, probate records document that Abner Jr., age 13, was a student at the Bastrop Military Institute in Bastrop, Texas. The 1861, Texas Almanac[40] listed R.T.P. Allen as the Superintendent with Governor Sam

---

[38] Brazoria County Deed: 1855, G-182
[39] Strobel, Page 23
[40] Texas Almanac, 1861, Page 303

Houston as the Chairman of the Board. Classes started on the first Monday in September and continued for forty weeks without intermission. Vacation was in July and August. Fees for tuition, board, lights, fuel and washing were $93 for elementary students and $115 for all others. The advertisement assured that the course of study would be unusually full, instruction thorough, and discipline strict.

The Jackson's oldest child, Arsenath, attended school in Columbia, Tennessee.[41] Sarah Ann Groce Wharton, the wife of William H. Wharton, owners of Eagle Island Plantation, also attended school in Columbia.[42] The Female Institute of Columbia charged $8 for a term of five months for beginning students, $12 for intermediate students, and $20 for advanced learning in reading, writing, grammar, geography, arithmetic, history, mythology, rhetoric, and philosophy. For additional sums, students could study a foreign language, $10; learn to play the harp, $30; learn organ, piano or guitar, $25; use of harp or piano for practicing, $5; use of organ or guitar for practicing, $2.50; drawing or painting lessons, $10; fancy work of every description, $10; riding lessons, $10; and $1 for pens, ink, ink stands, slates and pencils. Sunday lessons included the Bible, the Church Catechism, and conversations on the truth of the Christian religion.[43]

In October 1855, Abner and Margaret Jackson's only daughter married Jared Fulton Groce, son of Leonard W. Groce, at the Lake Jackson Plantation. The local newspaper, Democrat and Planter, of Columbia, Texas, had the following news about the wedding in their Tuesday, October 9, 1855 edition.

---

[41] Strobel, Page 43
[42] William H. Wharton had a sister, Elizabeth, who married Gilbert Bray Washington of Nashville, Tennessee. Their daughter, Elizabeth, married Lewis Strobel, son of Margaret Jackson Strobel.
[43] Platter, 1961 page 96

> Married
>
> At the residence of Maj. Abner Jackson
> in this County on the 4th inst, by Rev. M. C. Conoly,
> J. Fulton Groce of Austin County,
> to Miss Arsenath M. Jackson of this County.
> Thus has one of the fairest flowers of old Brazoria been plucked, but
> yet to bloom no doubt still fairer in her new home and sphere. May
> the lot of the newly married pair be one of life long happiness.

They made their home in Waller County and had five children. Their first child, Courtney Ann, died at the age of 4 in 1861; Abner Jackson Groce, died in 1914 leaving no descendants; George Fulton Groce also died in 1914 leaving no descendants; Courtney Fulton Groce married Horace Russell in 1882 and had a daughter named Eva Lee; Margaret Andrew Groce married Cole Wood and had a daughter Arsenath Jackson Wood.[44] Arsenath was the only one of the Jackson children to marry.

In 1856, because of the "shifting sand bar at the mouth of the Brazos, which caused repeated wrecks and damage and costly delays,"[45] Brazoria planters and Houston merchants secured a charter for the Houston Tap and Brazoria Railway Company to provide a rail connection with Brazoria and Houston. The rail would "tap into" the B.B.B. & C. Line (Buffalo Bayou, Brazos and Colorado) at Pierce Junction. By June 1857, 25 miles had been completed with planters providing free labor and materials. Stockholders included almost every planter in Brazoria Co.[46] The 1861, Texas Almanac reported that The Houston Tap and Brazoria Railroad

---

[44] Groce Family Records
[45] Creighton, 1975 Page 211
[46] Ibid, Pages 213-214

was complete and operational to Columbia. They referred to it as the "sugar road" as its chief function was to transport sugar out of Brazoria County.[47]

Abner Jackson wrote a check to Brazoria Railway Co. for $1000 on January 1, 1859.[48] The first record of goods shipped by Jackson is a receipt[49] from the Tap Rail Road for 22 half barrels of molasses ($154 minus $27.41 for shipping charges, to net, $126.59) on the 19th of November, 1860. During the Civil War, because metal was so precious, the tracks were removed and made into revolvers by the Dance brothers. Wooden rails were used but by the end of the war, the railroad was considered unsafe.[50]

On January 7, 1857, Margaret Jackson died. The division of her property and the final probate of her will continued until 1873. According to documents on file in the probates of Abner Jackson and Margaret Jackson, Abner Jackson asked his children, at the time of Margaret's death, not to claim their inheritance because he needed the estate intact for purposes of expansion. This agreement included Lewis M. Strobel, Magaret's son by her first marriage.

Abner Jackson continued the expansion of his holdings. On the 24th of February 1857, Jackson borrowed $20,000 from John A. Sauters.[51]

This borrowing and mortgaging of property was to acquire the Darrington Plantation that Jackson purchased for $116,200 in 1857 from the estate of Sterling McNeel.[52] Darrington lies about five miles north of the community of China Grove, Texas.

Abner J. Strobel, in his narratives, gave this description of Darrington.

---

[47] Texas Almanac, 1861 Edition, Page 228
[48] Jackson Probates: Folder 4, Item 1
[49] Ibid: Folder 4, Item 4
[50] Creighton, 1975 Page 215
[51] Jackson Probate Records, Folder 4, Item 281
[52] Brazoria County Deed: 1857, H-159

This [Darrington] was the plantation home of Sterling McNeel, and developed by him into a fine sugar plantation. Its sugar house was built of brick, and had a double set of kettles. The residence was a substantial frame building, also the cabins for the slaves. There were four of these McNeel brothers, J. Greenville, Sterling, Leander and Pleasant McNeel, and a cousin, Pinckney McNeel, all from Tennessee. Three of these brothers were in the battle of Velasco and Pleasant and his cousin Pinckney McNeel were in the battle of San Jacinto.... Upon the death of Sterling McNeel, the handsome property was purchased by Major Abner Jackson, and remained a part of his estate for several years after the war between the States. It is now [1926] owned and operated as a part of the prison system of farms, and is one of their finest plantations. The old slave time improvements have long since disappeared. The sugar house, an immense brick structure, was burned many years ago, and it is operated as a cotton plantation mainly.[53]

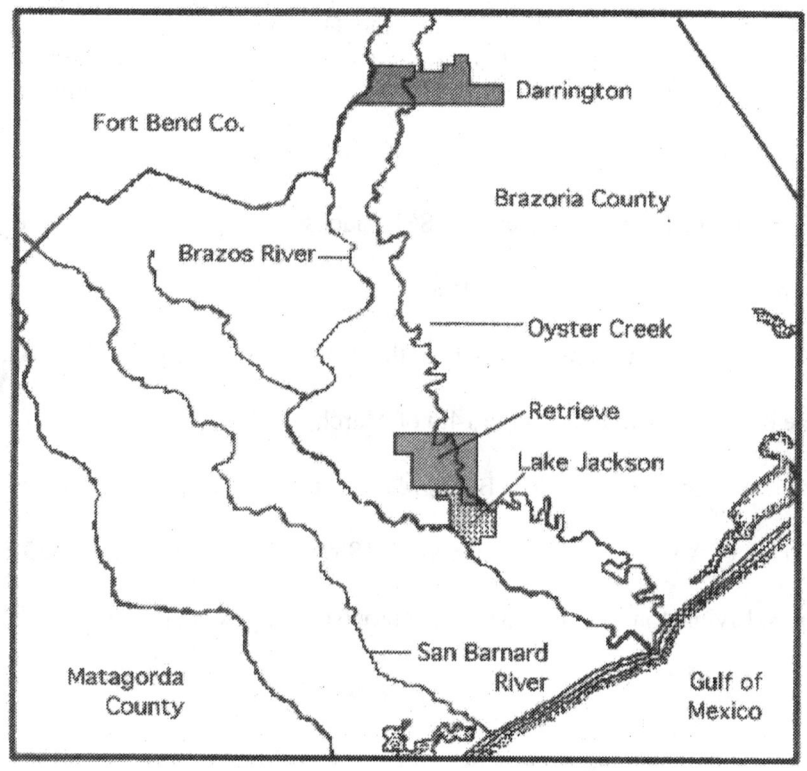

The Three Jackson Plantations

---

[53] Strobel, 1926

The sugar mill at the Jackson Plantation before 1858 was upgraded with the addition of a steam engine. That year 90 hogsheads of sugar were produced. An 1858 article in the *,Democrat and Planter,* Columbia, Texas, related the travels of a reporter as he visited the sugar mills on the east side of the Brazos River:

> Leaving the Bynum place we crossed Baileys prairie and visited the Retrieve. Here we found our young friend Andrew Jackson [age about 18] in charge. He was in the midst of a breakdown not one of those fancy breakdowns so common at this season of the year, on Oyster Creek, but some unfortunate accident to the mill. But we learned that it was not a very serious one, however, and they would be able to fire up again in a few hours. After partaking of an excellent dinner at the sugar house, we took a peep into the purgery, where we found some 250 hogsheads of good sugar. We were informed that the crop on the place would amount to about 400. Passing down toward Lake Jackson, we met our old friend the Major [Abner Jackson]. He informed us that on his three places, the Darrington, the Retrieve and Home Place [Lake Jackson Plantation], he would make about 900 [sic: 90 were actually produced] hogsheads, a right smart chance of sweetening for one man to put up.[54]

Between 1859 and the time of his death in 1861, "Jackson continued to buy slaves, issued mortgages at an amazing rate."[55] G. Ball and Robert Mills stated in a court document in 1862, that "Major Jackson was not considerably in debt at the death of M. [Margaret] Jackson..."[56] After her death, he borrowed heavily. On the 14th of March, 1859, Jackson borrowed $9000 from Hamilton P. Bee.[57] On Dec. 21, 1861, Bee sold the note to C. H. Stevens.[58] (This was three months after the death of Abner Jackson.) On April 9, 1859 Jackson borrowed $7,333.33 and 1/3 cents from Robert S. Livingstone.[59] This was also an outstanding debt at the time of his death.

---

[54] Brazosport Archaeological Society Newsletter, Vol. 13, #11, August 1994
[55] Brazoria County Deed: 1859, J-89, 118, 185, Survey Report 89-01, Page 8
[56] Jackson Probate Records, Folder 5, Item 9
[57] Ibid, Folder 4, Item 129
[58] Ibid, Folder 4, Item 130
[59] Ibid, Folder 3, Item 30

On February 1, 1860, Jackson borrowed $150 from A. Fox.[60] On February 10, 1860, it appears that he refinanced a loan of $55,000 he owed Robert Mills. He put up slaves by name for collateral.[61] On June 27th, 1860, Jackson borrowed $8000 from Tomkins and MacMurphy agreeing to pay back the sum in five months with an interest of 9% per annum.[62] On January 1, 1861, Jackson borrowed $823.23 at 8% interest from Wm. M. Brown.[63] On February 15, 1861, Jackson signed a series of ten notes to Ball Hutchins and Co. of Galveston.[64] It is assumed that this was for a loan of $10,000 dollars. He agreed to repay the loan in 10 payments in six months intervals beginning with September of 1862. Each payment was for $1200. Jackson's signature on these notes is very feeble.

The 1860 Census of Brazoria County, Texas, lists Abner Jackson with a real estate value of $84,415 and a personal estate valued at $88,360. Also listed were 285 slaves, 2550 acres under cultivation, 21,500 bushels of corn, 1900 bushels of potatoes, 622 bales of cotton, and 586 hogsheads of sugar. These numbers do not reflect that he owned a total of 10,727 acres: 4428 at Darrington, 4642 at Lake Jackson and his one half interest at Retrieve of 1,637 acres. Plus, small plots scattered in other locations. At the three plantations, in three herds, he owned approximately 2300 head of cattle.

On December 24, 1860, in New Orleans, Louisiana, Abner entered a marriage contract with Sarah Brownlee of South Carolina.[65] This contract, which kept their properties separate, is in the Appendices. Sarah Catherine Murray Brownlee was the widow of Elizah Brownlee and

---

[60] Ibid, Folder 6, Item 307
[61] Ibid, Folder 1, Item 38
[62] Ibid, Folder 4, Item 113
[63] Ibid, Folder 4, Item 55
[64] Ibid, Folder 4, Item 280
[65] Survey Report 89-01, Page 8

the niece of Margaret Strobel Jackson.[66] Sarah had one adopted daughter, Victoria May. Sarah and Abner were married on Christmas day in New Orleans and they returned to South Carolina.

Later, Abner returned to Texas and Sarah remained in South Carolina to settle the estate of her late husband, Elizah Brownlee. There is no evidence that Sarah came to Texas during Abner's life. After Abner's death, she married John Calvin Moorer and they lived in South Texas.[67]

When the Civil War began, sons Andrew, George W., Abner Jr., and John C. joined the Confederacy. "John C. and his brother, Andrew Jackson, were members of the 8th Texas Cavalry, both being members of John. A. Wharton's Company."[68] John C. enlisted on September 7, 1861, with a rank of Private. Records show that he spent his time in the hospital in Nashville, Tennessee. He was discharged from service on December 29, 1861, "unfit for service" because of chronic diarrhea. He is described as 24 years old, born in South Carolina, 5 feet 10 inches tall, dark complexion, gray eyes, dark hair, occupation - planter.[69] "George W. Jackson served in some command east of the Mississippi. The youngest son, Abner Jackson, a boy of 18 [sic -14] years[70], served west of the Mississippi, and died in the army and is buried in Arkansas."[71] Other records indicate that Abner, Jr. died in 1862 (at the age of 15) and Andrew in 1865.[72]

---

[66] Margaret Jackson had a brother, Baltis, Jr., who married Mary Stokes. Their daughter was Mary Ann who married John Soule Murray whose child was Sarah Catherine Murray who married Elizah Brownlee. Elizah died in 1859. Personal correspondence with Pat Johnson, descendent of Margaret Jackson.
[67] Personal correspondence with Pat Johnson, descendent of Margaret Jackson.
[68] Strobel, Page 43
[69] Army of the Confederate States, Certificate of Disability for Discharge, Signed Dec. 29, 1861, by [signature illegible].
[70] Abner Jr. was 14 years old in 1861.
[71] Stroble, Page 43
[72] Survey Report 89-01, Page 8

The Galveston Tribune Weekly of August 27, 1861, reported, "We learn from Col. Forshey, who arrived here on Friday evening from Velasco, that Maj. Abner Jackson, an old and highly respected citizen and wealthy planter of Brazoria County, died on Monday morning, the 21st inst., of congestive chills. He was sick only a few days. His wife, we learn, is with friends in South Carolina, and the only part of the family at home are three sons, two of whom had joined the company being raised by Hon. John R. Wharton, and were expected to leave for Virginia in a few days." Clinton Terry began signing letters administrating the estates of Abner and Margaret Jackson on September 17, 1861, and was responsible for the administration of the three plantations; Lake Jackson, Retrieve, and Darrington.

http://web.mac.com/joan_few

IV.

Family Tragedy: The Probate Years (1861- 1873)

The probate documents reveal the frustrations and conflicts between the Jackson siblings that led to the fatal confrontation between George and John.

Margaret Jackson died January 27, 1857 and Abner Jackson died August 21, 1861 in Brazoria County. Abner Jackson's will was never found and its absence may be related to the disinheritance of his oldest son, John C. Jackson.[1]

The probate records are located in files 764 and 765 in the Brazoria County Probate Records and contain over 900 documents stored in six folders. They contain the legal, economic, social and family history of this period. It took twelve years for the probate to be completed. During part of that time, John C. Jackson, served as executor of the estate. The conflict over the estate between the Jackson siblings led to the murder of John by his brother, George.

The first document indicating that the estate was going into probate was filed on September 17, 1861 when Clinton Terry appeared before the Brazoria Probate Court for letters of administration for the estate of Abner Jackson.[2] On October 1, 1861, Clinton Terry brought forth a $400,000 bond to secure his position as administrator of the estate of Margaret Jackson[3] and a bond of $750,000 dollars to be the administrator of Abner Jackson's estate. Signing with Terry as securities were John A. Wharton, John H. Herndon, John W. Brooks, A. J. Terry, S. S.

---

[1] Stroble, 1926
[2] Jackson Probate Records, Folder 2, Item 2
[3] Ibid, Folder 5, Item 2

McNees, L. S. Perry, and A. S. Lathrop.[4] Wharton, Terry and Masterson were attorneys at law in Houston and Wharton, Texas. Terry had a law office in Brazoria. They advertised in the 1860 Texas Almanac that they practiced in the Courts of the First Judicial District, and in the Supreme and Federal Courts of the State.[5]

October and November were the months when the sugar mills began processing sugar and Terry immediately began supervising the operations. On October 25, 1861, J. C. Hallet presented a bill for work done on cisterns and kettles.[6] [Probably Darrington Plantation kettles.] On November 4, Terry sold 1 hogshead and 10 barrels of sugar from Darrington for a total of $140.68.[7]

On November 12, 1861, an inventory was recorded for the estates of Margaret and Abner Jackson.[8] Abner Jackson's estate was valued at approximately $319,016 and Margaret's estate at $201,700.[9] The debts against both estates amounted to $105,691.20.

During November and December, Terry sold 44 hogsheads of sugar, 115 barrels of molasses and 23 one half barrels of molasses.[10] This produce was sold to different cotton factors for different prices. The hogsheads sold for between $50 to $100 dollars, with the molasses barrels from $12 to $13 dollars each. In comparison, planters got about $40 per hogshead in 1852.[11]

---

[4] Ibid Folder 2, Item 1
[5] 1860 Texas Almanac, Page 309
[6] Jackson Probate Records, Folder 6, Item 310
[7] Ibid, Folder 4, Item 26
[8] Ibid, Folders 2 and 5, Items 4
[9] Ibid, Folder 5, Item 4
[10] Ibid, Folder 4, Items 13,27,19,21,5,22,20,24,175,23, and 25, Folder 6, Items 4 and 5, and Folder 2, Item 9
[11] Creighton, James A., "A Narrative History of Brazoria County," Brazoria County Historical Commission, Printed by Texian Press, Waco, 1975, pp. 207

Most plantations finished their harvesting and processing of sugar cane before Christmas. In 1861, Darrington plantation must have finished by December 13. On that date, Terry paid Abner McMurty Jr. $260 for services of boiler for the sugar crop at Darrington Plantation for the year 1861.[12]

On the 23rd of December, Terry made an agreement with Robert and David Mills to deliver all the cotton bales from the Lake Jackson Plantation (about 80 bales) and the Darrington plantation (about 100 bales) to Mills as partial payment against debt owed Mills by the Abner and Margaret Jackson estates. The sale price was set at eight cents per pound.[13] In 1852, cotton averaged about eleven cents per pound[14] and between 1850 and 1860, averaged about 11.61 cents per pound for "middling cotton."[15] The Mills brothers were the largest sugar producers in Texas and cotton factors in Galveston. They advertised in the Texas Almanac of 1861 as "Cotton Factors and General Commission Merchants, Dealers in Money and in Foreign and Domestic Exchange."[16]

On December 30, an account statement from Cox Ennis and Co., Cotton Factors in Galveston, lists all items purchased for the estates and the barrels of molasses and sugar subtracted from the account between March 21 and December 15, 1861.[17]

Terry also paid various sums to heirs. On March 6, 1862, Abner Jackson Jr. recorded that, "At various time since my father's death Mr. Terry has handed me money amounting in all up to

---

[12] Jackson Probate Records, Folder 4, Item 2
[13] Ibid, Folder 6, Item 3
[14] Creighton, 1975, pp. 207
[15] Ibid, pp. 217
[16] Texas Almanac, 1861, pp. 284
[17] Jackson Probate Records, Folder 4, Item 50

this date to thirty dollars."[18] Jan. 23, 1862, shortly after returning from Tennessee with a medical discharge, John C. Jackson borrowed $120 from the estate.[19]

On January 1, 1862, Clinton Terry was paid $160.60 for his services to the estate.[20]

During January and February of 1862, Terry sold about 98 barrels of molasses at $10 to $13 dollars a barrel and 32 hogsheads of sugar at $75 to $100 dollars per hogshead. On February 19, Terry transferred to Tompkins, molasses barrels with a value of $8,079.06.[21] Abner Jackson had borrowed money from Tompkins and MacMurphy in 1860. "Five months after date (June 27, 1860) I promise to pay to the order of Tompkins and MacMurphy $8000. for value received, with interest from date at the rate of 9% per annum."[22]

In March, Terry paid $500 to W. T. Ballinger and T. G. Masterson, for attorney's fees for the administration of the estates of A. & M. Jackson.[23]

On April 14, 1862, Clinton Terry died and John C. Jackson petitioned the court to become administrator of the estates of Margaret and Abner Jackson.[24] On April 30, 1862, L. M. Stroble, son of Margaret Stroble Jackson, petitioned the Court to be Administrator Pro Tem for the Estates of Margaret and Abner Jackson.[25] On May 10, L. M. Stroble requested that the Court appoint Aurelius J. Terry as administrator of the estates.[26] On that same day, a bond was posted by Aurelius J. Terry to be the administrator of the estate of Abner Jackson[27] and to act as

---

[18] Ibid, folder 4, Item 42
[19] Ibid, Folder 4, Item 126
[20] Ibid, Folder 6, Item 128
[21] Ibid, Folder 4, Item 114
[22] Ibid, Folder 4, Item 113
[23] Ibid, Folder 4, Item 39
[24] Ibid, Folder 5, Item 6
[25] Ibid, Folder 5, Item 5
[26] Ibid, Folder 2, Item 10
[27] Ibid, Folder 4, Item 6

Administrator Pro Tem.[28] On May 17, 1862, Arsenath J. Groce and J. F. Groce requested the Court to appoint Aurelius J. Terry, administrator of the estates of Margaret and Abner Jackson.[29]

On May 21, L. M. Stroble again wrote to the County Court of Brazoria County recommending the appointment of Aurelius Terry as administrator of the estates of Margaret and Abner Jackson.[30] On May 23, Terry paid the Confederate War Tax of $1439.40, levied against the estates[31] which implies that he was acting as Administrator.

Why John's siblings did not want him to administer their parent's estate is never stated, but Abner Jackson Strobel, step grandson to Abner Jackson, related in his narrative history that, "Under the terms of Maj. Jackson's will his son John had been disinherited, but the will disappeared and was never probated."[32]

On May 26, John C. Jackson posted a bond of $300,000 to be administrator of the estate of Margaret Jackson.[33] On May 26, Ball Hutchings Co. of Galveston urged the Court to appoint Aurelius J. Terry as the administrator of the estate of Abner Jackson stating that the estate owed the Company $60,000.[34] On June 1, Terry purchased salt for the Darrington Place for the amount of $57.22.[35] On June 9, John C. Jackson paid A. J. Terry $800 for a payment of estate debt.[36] On July 1, a payment was made of $9,837.19 for the balances of credit of Clinton Terry, Administrator, and balance of credit to A.J. Terry Administrator, along with A. Sessums.[37]

---

[28] Ibid, Folder 1, Item 35
[29] Ibid, Folder 4, Item 138
[30] Ibid, Folder 4, Item 10
[31] Ibid, Folder 4, Item 186
[32] Stroble, 1926, Page 45
[33] Jackson Probate Records, Folder 5, Item 3
[34] Ibid, Folder 2, Item 7
[35] Ibid, Folder 4, Item 196
[36] Ibid, Folder 4, Item 202
[37] Ibid, Folder 4, Item 38

On the same day, John C. Jackson submitted an inventory of Abner Jackson's estates (in the Appendices). He gave the value of Abner Jackson's estate as $319,016. Also on July 1, John C. Jackson filed a separate document which gave the estate of Margaret Jackson to be valued at $154,710.[38]

This account by John does not match the inventory of Margaret Jackson's estate that was filed on November 12, 1861. That inventory states that the Community Property owned with Abner Jackson included:

1/2 Retrieve Plantation (3400 acres)	(no amount given)
Retrieve Stock of cattle (800 head)	$4800
160 acres near Liverpool	$100
Lot #7 in St. Louis	$10
Lake Jackson Plantation (2535 acres)	(no amount given)
Lake Jackson Negroes	(no amount given)

Total Value of Margaret Jackson estate: $201,770.

The question of what was to be included in community property, became an issue of vital importance to Arsenath Jackson Groce, her husband, Fulton Groce, L. M. Stroble, Andrew Jackson, George W. Jackson and Abner Jackson, Jr. The lawsuits against John C. Jackson began.

Between July 1, and the end of October 1862, L. M. Stroble brought seven legal actions against John Jackson.[39] During these litigations, John continued to administer the estates. He petitioned the courts to allow him to sell crops at private sale. The petition states that, "The estate of Abner Jackson owns the Darrington Plantation and one half interest in the Retrieve Plantation and a community interest of one half in the Lake Jackson Plantation and the estate of Margaret Jackson, deceased, owns a community interest of one half in the Lake Jackson

---

[38] Ibid, Folder 5, Item 8
[39] Ibid, Folder 1, Items 3,2,10,6,11; Folder 4, Item 30; Folder 5, Item 10

Plantation.[40] During this time there must have been a hearing or trial concerning the questions of community property of Margaret Jackson. On October 27, Asinith [sic] Groce, Fulton Groce, L. M. Stroble, Andrew Jackson, George W. Jackson, Abner Jackson, Jr., James P. Bigham and S.A. Towsy put up securities of $78,000, to cover the debts against the estate of Margaret Jackson.[41]

On August 30, L. M. Stroble brought this request before the Court, "In this case the plaintiff by his attn. [attorney] moves the court to grant him a new trial for the following reasons ... he believes he can prove that Major A. Jackson agreed with L. M. Stroble and Mrs. Groce that if they would consent for him the said Jackson to hypothecate the community property to raise money to purchase the Darrington place and other property that said purchases should insure to the benefit of the community and should be considered as community property ... [also] since the trial of said Court learned that he can prove that the Negroes were purchased before the death of Margaret Jackson and should be returned as community property."[42] On the same day this petition was filed, T. Lynch Hamilton gave oath to the Court that two slaves, the boy, Jeffe[sp?], and the woman, Margaret, were purchased before the death of Margaret Jackson.[43] There are no records in the probate files which document the settlement of the estate of Margaret Jackson following her death. All records refer to estate actions after the death of Abner Jackson.

On December the 24, 1862, John C. Jackson filed a complaint objecting to the County Commissioners inventory of the estates. He states that the count of Negroes, mules and teams is

---

[40] Ibid, Folder 2, Item 12
[41] Ibid, Folder 2, Item 11
[42] Ibid, Folder 1, Item 11
[43] Ibid, Folder 5, Item 11

wrong because Lake Jackson and Retrieve plantations are community property and the inventory was not divided to represent the estate of Margaret Jackson.[44]

On December 29, the Commissioners outlined the procedure for dividing the Negroes, mules and oxen of the two estates. The slaves belonging to Margaret and Abner Jackson were valued at $58,000. To divide the slaves, two lots were drawn. Lot one, valued at $28,950, designated as the estate of Abner Jackson. Lot two, valued at $29,100, the estate of Margaret Jackson. From lot two, the Negroes were then divided into 6 equal lots (of near equal value); lot 1 to Andrew Jackson, lot 2 to George Jackson, lot 3 to L. M. Stroble, lot 4 to John Jackson, lot 5 to Abner Jackson, Jr., and lot 6 to Aseneth [sic] Groce (It mentions that some Negroes had previously been advanced to Mrs. Aceneth [sic] Groce). Mules and oxen were listed by name and value and were again divided into two lots representing the two estates. From lot 2, Margaret Jackson estate, the animals were divided into six lots, as financially equal as possible. The six heirs drew the lots. Other property was listed, but was not divided, because land and crops could not be divided equally.[45]

On the same day, Arsnith [sic] Groce, L. M. Stroble, Andrew, George, and Abner Jr., Jackson, objected to the Commissioners division of the estate, "And for further answer they wave that Andrew [slave] who was allotted to the Estate of Abner Jackson is the best sugar boiler on the Lake Place and that he is also a good carpenter. That Abraham [slave] is a good cooper and Jim [slave] is a good foreman or driver and that they were also allotted to Abner Jackson Estate."[46]

---

[44] Ibid, Folder 5, Item 12
[45] Ibid, Folder 5, Item 13
[46] Ibid, Folder 4, Item 33

The heirs began to rent, swap and loan slaves to each other. In March of 1863, John agreed to pay Abner Jackson, Jr., $950 for the use of his slaves for one year.[47] He also purchased, for $1000, the mules, horses and oxen allotted to G.W. Jackson and Abner Jackson, Jr. in the division of Margaret Jackson's estate.[48] George traded with John the Negro Caldwell for the Negro boy Calif.[49] Later in June, John purchased for $1200, 12 young horses from Abner Jr.[50] In September, John rented some of his slaves to the estate of Margaret Jackson for a yearly sum of $900, and rented 8 of his slaves (Frank, 30; Scott, 27; Joe, 35; Polly, 30; Peter, 40; Malinda, 25; Aggi, 18; Margaret, and Ducey) to the estate of Abner Jackson for a sum of $5,840. On September 1, 1864, this rental amount was questioned. The legal request was "to appraise the hire of the following named Negroes [listed above] belonging to John C. Jackson which were hired to the estate of Abner Jackson deceased."[51] John also sold to the estate four cotton cards for a price of $600.[52]

About this time, John must have petitioned the Court to allow a division of the real estate belonging to the two estates in a similar way the slaves and stock had been divided. On April 2, 1863, the Commissioners responded, "We are of the opinion that said real estate can not be divided without manifest injury to the two estates and we do hereby adopt in this report the value of said real estate as it has been heretofore ascertained by us in the inventory of said estates as made out in the inventory heretofore turned into this court by John C. Jackson, Adms."[53] During

---

[47] Ibid, Folder 6, Item 275
[48] Ibid, Folder 6, Item 58
[49] Ibid, Folder 2, Item 17
[50] Ibid, Folder 4, Item 171
[51] Ibid, Folder 2, Item 33
[52] Ibid, Folder 6, Item 264
[53] Ibid, Folder 2, Item 15

this division of property, the debtors of the estates of M. and A. Jackson were clamoring for payment.

Cotton production on the Lake Jackson and Darrington plantations in the spring of 1863 totaled 168,760 pounds. At 8 cents a pound, this would be worth $13,500.

Cotton was very important to the Confederate cause. "Cotton taken overseas by such ships [blockade runners] would buy for the Confederates (hampered by lack of manufacturing facilities) guns, gunpowder, medicines, coffee, cloth, hardware, and shoes. Purchases came into Texas by the same route that cotton was freighted out."[54]

Confederate "Ships loaded with cotton entered waterways around Titlum-Tatlum [a small island near the upper entrance to San Luis Pass] and hid among the willows, out of range of observers with spyglasses on the tall masts of Federal blockading ships. On dark nights or in bad weather blockade runners would slip out of here to the open seas, hugging shores, being towed by men on land until deep water was reached."[55]

To protect the production of sugar and cotton, confederate troops were stationed at the mouth of the Brazos River and on plantations in the area. In March, Jackson sold 82 bushels of potatoes to the Confederate Army for $2 a bushel.[56] In April, a Captain W. Masters purchased for the Confederate Army 30 bushels of corn for $45.[57] In October, a Capt. Daniel Richardson purchased 11 beeves at $60 each for the Confederates.[58]

---

[54] Creighton, 1975, pp. 241
[55] Ibid, pp. 240
[56] Jackson Probate Records, Folder 6, Item 212
[57] Ibid, Folder 4, Item 219
[58] Ibid, Folder 4, Item 221

In May of 1863, the estate sold 5 hogsheads of sugar for a gross of $2,007.99[59] which is a considerable increase from the $100 price per hogshead the estate was getting in 1862.

On May 7, 1863, a payment of debt of the estate of A. Jackson was paid to John Whereley. The payment was in goods: 270 barrels, 1 well bucket, 58 bushels of corn, 200 pounds sugar, 1 barrel of molasses for a total of $1,169.25.[60]

To further divide the estates among the heirs and to satisfy debtors, John attempted to sell the Lake Jackson Place and Retrieve. A notice of sale was posted on July 2, 1863.

> All that plantation known as Lake Jackson Place situated on Oyster Creek about seven miles from Brazoria, containing 3733 acres of land, 900 of which are in a high state of cultivation. Also a fine brick sugar house and first class Engine and Mill. Also a good Gin House and Grist Mill attached. Also a fine Brick Dwelling house and brick out houses all in fine condition. The above is one of the finest and most desirable plantations on Oyster Creek.
>
> At the same time and place the one undivided half interest of all that plantation known as the "Retrieve" situated on Oyster Creek about [?] given miles from Brazoria containing 3400 acres of land, about 1000 or 1100 acres of which are in a high state of cultivation. Also the one half interest in a fine Brick sugar house, swelling house and all other improvements on the said plantation.
>
> Terms of the sale. Credit of 12 months, notes with good personal security and a mortgage on the property to secure the payment of the purchase money.
>
> Possession of the property to be given on the 1st day of January, 1864.
>
> Brazoria, April 28, 1863   John C. Jackson, Admn.[61]

---

[59] Ibid, Folder 4, Item 159
[60] Ibid, Folder 2, Item 38
[61] Ibid, Folder 2, Item 20

The May, June and July account ledgers with A. Sessums & Co. lists purchases and payments made in Confederate Notes.[62] This is the first notation in the records of Confederate currency being used.

During the summer of 1863, the people of Brazoria County began to feel a lack of supplies. Flour and coffee were "practically non-existent" and many women found themselves running plantations while their husbands were at war.[63]

In August, John Jackson sold 8 hogsheads to Ball Hutchings & Co. for a net of $3,838.32 and five days later, sold an additional 12 hogsheads. On the 23rd, he bought a "fine gray Stallion, six years old" for the estate for which he paid $1,200, in full.[64] On the 13th of September, John purchased a young gray stallion for the estate for a price of $875.[65] These gray stallions were purchased "for the estate" at a time when debtors were in line to be paid.

On September 1, 1863, John applied to the Court to be able to sell household and kitchen furniture belonging to the estate; "...there is on the Lake Jackson Plantation a considerable quantity of Household and Kitchen furniture and that the same is the community property of the said estate of Abner and Margaret Jackson Deceased. [On this document, the word "community" has been drawn through and the word "separate" written over it and the word "Margaret" has been drawn through leaving only to read the estate of Abner Jackson.] That this plantation has been sold and that it would be to the interest of said estates [here the "s" has been scratched out] to sell all the household and kitchen furniture on said place...." Signed Lathrop McCormick,

---

[62] Ibid, Folder 4, Item 217
[63] Creighton, 1975, pp. 247
[64] Jackson Probate Records, Folder 4, Item 222
[65] Ibid, Folder 4, Item 243

Attn. for petitioners.[66] Brazoria County Deed Record K - 362, records that on June 8, 1863, Andrew and Abner Jackson [Jr.] sold to C. Stringfellow, 1/2 interest in Jackson Place for $38,500.

On August 28th, John paid $750 in attorney's fees from the estates.[67] It appears that the fees were for the defense of John in the various lawsuits against him.

On September 1, 1863, John presented to the Court an Annual Exhibit which lists everything sold by the estates between October 8, 1862 and August 15, 1863.[68]

On the 12th, John sold from the Lake Jackson plantation:

> 22 Bales of Cotton to Peaburn and Lawson for $1941.20
> 1272 bushels of corn
> 85 lbs of old copper
> corn and potatoes sold in small parcels to different persons,
> 1 copper kettle to Chironje weighing 526 lbs
> lbs of sugar to different people in weights between 50-100 lbs
> butter
> 6 slaves hired to J.H. Herdon for 33 days at $2.50 for $82.50.[69]

On October 10, 1863, a notice for the sale of household and kitchen goods for the Lake Jackson plantation was posted.[70] On September 22, Andrew Jackson made an inventory of the household and kitchen items in the Lake Jackson house. His estimate of the inventory was $1,706.05.[71] On that day, a public sale was held. Purchasers and items purchased were:

> Thomas G. Masterson: wine glasses, rifle, linen sheets, bed spread,
> table cloths, napkins, mattresses, quilts, lot of dishes, trunk,

---

[66] Ibid, Folder 2, Item 21
[67] Ibid, Folder 4, Item 256
[68] Ibid, Folder 5, Item 14
[69] Ibid, Folder 4, Item 106
[70] Ibid, Folder 2, Item 25
[71] Ibid, Folder 6, Item 57

curtains, etc.   Total $140.35[72]

Purchaser Unknown: furniture, goblets, medicine scales, quilts, book, 9 Vol. set Encyclopedia, etc.   Total $191.70[73]

Purchaser Unknown: curtains, mattress, books, etc. Total $43.50[74]

Purchaser Unknown: furniture, quilts, books, bedding, glasses, etc. Total $327.50[75]

C.R. Cox: 3 quilts for $55, plates, mattresses, pillows, sheets, bed spread, table spread, etc..   Total $133.50[76]

Dr. Broadnax: goblets, bedstead, mattresses, 2 Vol. Scott's Bible, wash stand and pitcher, hide bottom chairs, linens, etc.   Total $93[77]

Purchaser Unknown: 1 chair, soap dish and cup, 1 picture "Niagara," 9 soup plates, 1 picture.   Total $35[78]

J. Sheath: 1 pair L. P. slips, 1 bureau, 1 book, 2 L. towels, one small trunk, Total $23.75[79]

In November, John paid $3,426.21 in County and State taxes for the estate for the year 1863.[80] An additional receipt shows $192.64 which may have been his personal taxes.[81]

Early in November of 1863, Federal forces swept up the Texas coast from the south, until they occupied Matagorda Island just south of the Brazos River.[82] Because of this threat, Confederate forces (approximately 391 officers and 5,234 solders[83]) were concentrated in the Brazoria County area.[84] In March of 1864, Major General John A. McClernand of the Union

---

[72] Ibid, Folder 4, Item 204
[73] Ibid, Folder 4, Item 195
[74] Ibid, Folder 4, Item 197
[75] Ibid, Folder 4, Item 201
[76] Ibid, Folder 6, Item 156
[77] Ibid, Folder 4, Item 214
[78] Ibid, Folder 4, Item 62
[79] Ibid, Folder 4, Item 157
[80] Ibid, Folder 4, Item 234
[81] Ibid, Folder 4, Item 212
[82] Creighton, 1975, pp. 243
[83] Ibid, pp. 245
[84] Ibid, pp. 244

Army announced that all his forces had been transferred to Matagorda Island.[85] The people of Brazoria County expected the worst but, in April, the Union forces left Matagorda and joined the Red River expedition,[86] the Red River being another very important cotton producing area of Texas.

On November 22, John Jackson made a donation of $50 of behalf of the estate to the Soldiers Great Society.[87] A few days later, 12 hogsheads were sold from Darrington.[88] On the 30th, the estate paid the Confederate State Taxes for the year 1863; 1,280 gallons molasses, 15,032 pounds of sugar (about 15 hogsheads) and 800 bushels of corn.[89]

In December, the estate sold to the Confederates, 170 bushels of corn for $233.75[90] and a black horse to Col. Lyken's Regiment for $100.[91]

The year 1864 began with payments and settlements of 1863 expenses. Henry Hudging received $1,500, for "boiling the sugar crop of the Darrington plantation for the year 1863."[92]

On the 7th of January, the Confederate Army requested 50 bushels of corn.[93] On the 10th, the army received from Andrew Jackson 3 barrels of molasses and 1 hogshead of sugar. It was received by a Captain D. C. Richardson at Sandy Point, Texas.[94] On the 26th, Confederate taxes were paid for the year 1862, at $1,594.[95]

---

[85] Ibid, pp. 245
[86] Ibid
[87] Jackson Probate Records, Folder 6, Item 244
[88] Ibid, Folder 6, Item 207
[89] Ibid, Folder 6, Items 181 and 209
[90] Ibid, Folder 6, Item 229
[91] Ibid, Folder 4, Item 258
[92] Ibid, Folder 4, Item 209
[93] Ibid, Folder 6, Item 266
[94] Ibid, Folder 6, Item 119
[95] Ibid, Folder 4, Item 236

In February, the estate paid John Lang $3,234.65 for his services between July 5, 1862 and February 10, 1864[96] [As overseer at Darrington]. Another amount of $916.63 was paid on April 1, "for wages on Darrington in full of all demands up to the 1st. day of Jan. 1864."[97] Lang received $920 as overseer for the year 1864.[98]

Salt was purchased on the 11th from Alfred C. McKeen & Co. for $233. On the 15th, 6 bales of cotton were shipped to A. Sessums Co. for a net of $418.[99] Payment was made in gold coin.[100]

During the first three months of 1864, John Jackson sold for the estate, approximately 17 hogsheads for about $170 each, 119 barrels of molasses at $232 each and 6 bales of cotton for $70 each.[101]

On the 26th of March, A. J. Sessums Co. did a money conversion. $7,700 in Confederate money was converted to coin at 37 for 1 to equal $210. Charges of $13.10 were subtracted for a Balance in Specie of $196.90. It was signed by Alex Sessums.[102] On the same day, 6 hogsheads of sugar netted $3,478.20 in Confederate notes,[103] which converted would be $94 in specie, and 30 barrels of molasses sold for $6,936.[104] which converted to $187. On the 14th of May, 23 hogsheads were sold to T.W. House Cotton Factors for $64,378.43.[105] Assuming that this is Confederate dollars, converted to specie would be about $75 for each hogshead.

---

[96] Ibid, Folder 6, Item 233
[97] Ibid, Folder 6, Item 232
[98] Ibid, Folder 6, Item 271
[99] Ibid, Folder 4, Item 210
[100] Ibid, Folder 6, Item 249
[101] Ibid, Folder 4, Items: 286,238,279,239,275,285,288,278,284,269, and 268, Folder 6, Items 249 and 231
[102] Ibid, Folder 6, Item 278
[103] Ibid, Folder 6, Item 230
[104] Ibid, Folder 4, Item 271
[105] Ibid, Folder 4, Item 267

From this point in the records, not all receipts or bills distinguish between Confederate bills or specie. On the 6th of June, Confederate taxes were paid on livestock at $613.55[106] and a tax on income of $181.[107]

On the 13th of June, a receipt indicates that John was growing tobacco for sale. "Received from J. C. J. adm. est. A. Jackson deceased, $670 the same being due me on a portion of tobacco prepared for market by me on the shares for said estate - the tobacco was divided as far as was [able], 2/3 to the estate and 1/3 to me, but the number of boxes would not divide even and the difference was settled in money at $25 per pound," signed, J. I. Hopper.[108] On the 9th of September, a bill of sale from T.W. House & Co. shows that they purchased from J. C. J., 29 boxes of tobacco for a net of $12,136.[109]

On June 10, 1864, a settlement was made by J. C. J. to a John A. Sauters, "Received in produce $23,144 in full satisfaction of my claim against the estate."[110]

The next record documenting the division of the estate among the heirs occurs on August, 19, 1864. Andrew Jackson claimed [sold] his share of the Retrieve Plantation and received from Estate Administrator, J. C. Jackson, $7,700.[111]

On August 20, 1864, John petitioned the Court for a leave of absence, "...that the affairs of said estates are now in good condition and will not require his personal presence for some time. He therefore prays that your honor will grant him lean of absence from the state for six months

---

[106] Ibid, Folder 2, Item 224
[107] Ibid, Folder 4, Item 223
[108] Ibid, Folder 4, Item 254
[109] Ibid, Folder 6, Item 225
[110] Ibid, Folder 4, Item 281
[111] Ibid, Folder 6, Item 218

and for all such other orders as may be necessary in the present." This petition was signed by Lathrop McCormick, Attn. for J. C. Jackson.[112]

On September 1, 1864, a petition was brought before the Court concerning John's rental of his personal slaves, 8 total, to the estate of Abner Jackson for the amount of $5,840 for one year.[113]

On October 4, George W. Jackson petitioned the Court to be a party to the case now pending in which H. B. Cash is the plaintiff and J. C. Jackson is defendant as administrator of the estates of A. and M. Jackson. In the petition George states that the debts against said estate of Margaret Jackson have been paid. He also states that the estate of M. Jackson has a surplus of $6,834.84 that needs to be divided among the heirs.[114] On November 2, a petition was brought against John as administer of the estate of Abner Jackson. This document is very hard to read, but it appears to question the $25,966.29 balance on the estate and, "His account also shows that he has in his hands old issue of C.S. notes belonging to said estate of $70,000.49."[115]

During this last year of the Civil War, documents verify that business continued as usual with Confederate notes and coin (specie) as currency. On June 29, 1865, the Estate paid L. W. House $1,299.25 in Confederate Currency with a conversion of 62 at 40 to one or 2/2 ¢ on the dollar in specie.[116]

On August 1, 1865, John received a letter from Ball Hutchings Co. [factor and creditor], "We have herein the Account of Cotton showing a balance of $7,138.47, which we have placed

---

[112] Ibid, Folder 2, Item 31
[113] Ibid, Folder 2, Item 33
[114] Ibid, Folder 5, Item 24
[115] Ibid, Folder 3, Item 3
[116] Ibid, Folder 6, Item 112

as a credit on the Lake Jackson probate claim. We also have sent to Major Hamilton the Retrieve Account closed by canceling three notes each which we sent to him to be handed to you. How have you succeeded with the freedman? We hope that you will be able to have your present crop - What are your prospects? Cotton is very high and quotes 48 cents in New York."[117]

During the first six months of 1865, commerce continued using a variety of currency and barter. John Jackson sold for the estate: cotton at 8 cents per pound,[118] sugar, molasses, bacon, corn, fodder, and tobacco. A keg of molasses was selling for about $3.71.[119]

No probate records refer to the end of the war. It appears that Confederate currency was used during the summer of 1865, along with coin.

> The end of the Civil War and the period of Reconstruction which followed did nothing to alleviate the sugar planters' woes. Lack of competent labor, deterioration of equipment, the breakdown in ownership and management due to military losses, plus straitened [sic] finances - all contributed to the continued decline of the sugar industry. By 1869, Texas sugar production had dropped to 2,020 hogsheads, of which Brazoria County produced about 75 per cent, the rest being credited to sixteen other counties, with Fort Bend (302 hogsheads) standing next to Brazoria County.[120] By comparison, in 1858, Brazoria County produced 5,150 hogsheads.[121]

On November 3, 1865, the Court required John to post a new bond of $200,000 as administrator of the Estates of M. and A. Jackson.[122] On August 31, 1866, the Court of Brazoria County ordered John to appear at the September session of the Court about the new bond.[123] On September 11, another Court order was issued to John to appear at the September session.[124] On

---

[117] Ibid, Folder 6, Item 293
[118] Ibid, Folder 6, Item 263
[119] Ibid, Folder 6, Item 106
[120] Creighton, 1975, pp. 207
[121] Ibid, pp. 205
[122] Jackson Probate Records, Folder 5, Item 15
[123] Ibid, Folder 5, Item 18
[124] Ibid, Folder 2, Item 32

October 1, the County Court of Brazoria County issued a "Command to appear" to John about the new bond.[125] On October 26, H. L. B. Cash filed a petition against John Jackson.

> H. L. B. Cash, a citizen of Brazoria County, complaining of John C. Jackson, administrator of the Estate of Abner Jackson deceased, respectfully presents to your honor that by the purchase of the interest of one of the heirs to said Jackson, he has become interested in said estate, therefore he complains.
>
> Petitioner represents that the said John C. Jackson has managed the affairs in a negligent, careless and illegal manner, in this, he has not although more than 12 months have expired since said succession was opened, filed in court a correct list of all the claims against the estate and the condition of the claims, he has not made a full....[some of this document is missing].....
>
> Petitioner represents that he is informed and so charges that the said J. Jackson has withheld some of the means of produce of said estate and neglected to pay the debts when he might have paid them to great advantage to the estate.
>
> Cash ask that Jackson be cited and appear in Court to answer these complaints.[126]

In November, John was ordered to appear in County Court to "make an exhibit of the condition of said estate and answer complaint of H. L. B. Cash."[127] On January 4, 1867 the Court issued to John Jackson a, "Command to appear in County Court of Brazoria County to show cause why he has not obeyed Court orders;"[128] an additional summons to appear in Court with a new bond,[129] and a third summons to appear at the January term of the Court to make exhibit of the estates of M. and A. Jackson.[130] Later in January, another Court order summoned

---

[125] Ibid, Folder 5, Item 17
[126] Ibid, Folder 2, Item 45
[127] Ibid, Folder 2, Item 41
[128] Ibid, Folder 5, Item 19
[129] Ibid, Folder 5, Item 21
[130] Ibid, Folder 5, Item 20

John, "to show cause why he has not complied with and obeyed the order of the court at the May term last ordering him to pay a judgment entered up against them in favor of M. S. Munson ex. of the last will of A. Winters decd. otherwise he will be dismissed from the administration of the estate of A. Jackson, decd."[131]   On January 15, Louis M. Stroble wrote a letter to Judge S.W. Perkins of the Brazoria County Court,

> Dear Sir,
> I find that it is impossible for Wash Masterson and myself to give the required bond on father's estate. My name being the objectionable feature in the matter. I have therefore concluded to withdraw my name and most respectfully suggest Wm Masterson with T. W. I am satisfied that they can give the bond and will be both satisfactory to the creditors and heirs the condition of the estate is said that some immediate steps must be taken or everything will go to min.
> Respectfully, Louis M. Stroble[132]

On the 29th of January, 1867, John posted a bond of $260,000 dollars to be Administer of the estate of Abner Jackson. It was cosigned by A. J. Terry, A. Sessums, Aaron Coffee, H. [name illegible], John Lang, Lynch Hamilton, John Swany, J. W. Brookes, J. H. Laskeader, A. Underwood, C. F. Patten, Louis M. Stroble.[133]   On the 31st, John posted a bond for the estate of Margaret Jackson.[134]

In February, John was again summoned to Court to "answer to the complaints of petitioner H. L. B. Cash."[135]

---

[131] Ibid, Folder 2, Item 47
[132] Ibid, Folder 3, Item 8
[133] Ibid, Folder 2, Item 61
[134] Ibid, Folder 5, Item 44
[135] Ibid, Folder 2, Item 48

In March, John Jackson gave a sworn statement to the County that "T. L. Hamilton was to have charge and management of Retrieve. The estate of M. Jackson was one forth [sic] of Retrieve." The statement includes lists of expenses and payments at Retrieve.[136]

In April, Ball Hutchings Co., Cotton Factors in Galveston, brought their claims to the Court against the estate of A. Jackson. Abner Jackson borrowed money from Ball Hutchings in 1861 with the following payment due dates:

June 1, 1861	$5000
June 1, 1862	$5000
June 1, 1863	$5000
June 1, 1864	$5000
June 1, 1865	$5000
June 1, 1866	$900
Payments against debt:	
Dec. 1, 1863	$600
June 1, 1864	$600
Dec. 1, 1864	$300
June 1, 1865	$300

"All of which are levied by Trust Deed on Retrieve Plantation meeting above notes on record in Brazoria County."
"A Jackson note for J. S. Sanders by B. Hole, $1,200, secured on Lake Jackson Plantation."
"Account against Estate of A. Jackson approved on March 13, 1862, at $29,369.43, with credit by August 1, 1865, $7,138.47."
"All of the above claims allowed by the Administrator of said Estate and approved by Probate judge. Also on Record the contract agreement with John C. Jackson, dated April 1, 1866."[137]

On May 3, John submitted a ledger to the Court listing the debts paid against the estate of Abner Jackson. The total debt listed on the page was $30,913.60. Between Dec. 23, 1865, and

---

[136] Ibid, Folder 6, Item 22
[137] Ibid, Folder 6, Item 252

Dec. 23, 1866, $9,027.71 was paid against these debts.[138] On this same date, John submitted to the Court a written statement in reference to the condition of the estate of A. Jackson, deceased.

> He (John) shows that the year 1866 was one of unprecedented disaster to the cropping interest of this county. That he had a great many hands employed off and on during said year on the Darrington plantation but that he only succeeded in saving about 75 hogsheads of sugar and 125 barrels of molasses and syrup, and very little cotton, 25 bales of such he has shipped and sold and credited in his accounts and estimates there are 30 bales remaining.
>
> Petitioner hardly knows in which accounts to report the proceeds of Lake Jackson Plantation for reasons known to your[sic], but he shows that he leased said place to Kennicott and others and that on settlement with them he received 4 bales cotton and about 900 bushels of corn, that the cotton has been shipped through Thompson and McMurphy and is not yet reported sold........In regard to Retrieve Plantation that in addition to the ordinary or prevailing disaster to the cotton crop last season that the sugar crop was lost on the Retrieve by the explosion of the steam boilers connected with the sugar mill so injuring the machinery as to render it impossible to save the crop then on hand.
>
> The Lake Jackson Plantation mill figure with the estate of Andrew Jackson, deceased, but for the information of the court, petitioner states that he is employing about the number of 30 hands on the Lake Jackson plantation and considers his present prospect good for crops of corn and cotton.[139]

In September, George W. Jackson, again petitioned the Court to have the estate of Margaret Jackson partitioned and distributed. "G. W. Jackson states 12 months has passed since court order. Request that J. C. J. be cited to appear in Court and show why partition and distribution of estate among heirs has not taken place. States that J. C. J. has had time and funds to pay all debts of every kind against said estate that have been allowed and approved or established by suit."[140] The Court gave George W. Jackson ownership of the Lake Jackson Plantation.[141]

---

[138] Ibid, Folder 2, Item 50
[139] Ibid, Folder 2, Item 51
[140] Ibid, Folder 5, Item 23
[141] Brazoria County Deed: 1867, L-600

On October 1, 1867, H. L. B. Cash and G. W. J. [George W. Jackson] petitioned the Courts objecting to the exhibit of the condition of the estate of M. Jackson as made by the Administrator of the estate [John C. Jackson] on the 27th of March 1867. They list the following objections:

1. they see no reason why estate of M. J. can not be closed and partitioned.
2. object to charge of $4,500 because charge is not properly itemized.
3. 1st item on credit side of $1,756.60 is wrong.
4. $15,000 went through Ball Hutching & Co. that is not accounted for.
5. J. C. J. became administrator of M. J. estate on June 15, 1862. Produce is not accounted for and crops on the Lake Place for 1862 and 1863 are not accounted for.
6. stock cattle, hogs, farming equipment, bales of cotton and 15 hogsheads were sold by J. C. J. and not accounted for.
7. J. C. J. can not account for cotton and hogsheads that were in the trust of the previous administrator.
8. they charge that DeArey owed M. Jackson estate a large sum of money, the exact amount is not known and not accounted for.
9. Abner Jackson's death occurred in August of 1861. Between Margaret Jackson's death and A. J.'s death, A. J. used the proceeds of M. J.'s estate for his own use and J. C. J. has not made A. J. estate account for the use to the heirs of M a r g a r e t Jackson.
10. that the administrator of M. Jackson's estate [John Jackson] owes interest on "all sums improperly and wrongfully kept in his hands at the highest rate of legal interest."
11. object to the rent on Maclen [sic] place that was used by J. C. J. Amount to low.[142]

---

[142] Jackson Probate Records, Folder 5, Item 25

There is no record of when John received this petition of his brother's or if he responded to it. We do know the two brothers confronted each other at the Lake Jackson plantation on December 4, 1867. Abner Stroble described the tragedy:

> I will now relate the story of the tragedy in this family, so as to forever set to rest the garbled versions of the affair that are being circulated by those who are not familiar with the causes leading up to it, and did not even know the brothers. I will state that my father was their half-brother making me a nephew. I am the only living person who saw the killing and who is familiar with the events that led up to it. The killing of John C. Jackson by his brother, George W., occurred December 8, 1868 [court records give the date as Dec. 4, 1867], at Lake Jackson. When the war closed in 1865, my father went to Mexico and remained a year. George W. went with him and returned after a few months to Brazoria County. He was in feeble health, made so by his army life and when he came to Sandy Point where his brother, John C. had a store and lived on the Chebang Plantation near there in 1866, John being the administrator of his father's estate, George applied to John for funds so he could live, he being penniless and just out of the army.. The salutation he received from his brother John was to be knocked down with the loaded end of a quirt and quirted in public at Sandy Point. George took this, but ever after it wrankled in his bosom, and he avoided his brother John. In 1867 he [George] applied to the court for his portion of his father's property. The court set aside the Lake Jackson Plantation of 6,700 acres of land [sic- 4,642.55 acres[143]], the A. J. stock of cattle and 150 head of horses and mules as George's portion of the property. On December 8th, 1868 [court documents give the date as Dec. 4, 1867.] when the fatal tragedy occurred; John rode from the Darrington Plantation, another one of the plantations belonging to the estate, near Sandy Point, to Lake Jackson. This was the first time the brothers had met since John cowhided George. As they met on the walk leading to the residence, John remarked to George, "My young man, I want you to go to Brazoria today and sign some papers." George said,

---

[143] Court Probate Records and Maps

"John, remember who you are talking to - that you are not talking to a free negro." John said, "If you do not like it, Sir, I will cowhide you." When he made that remark, George shot him six times in the breast. Both were armed. In fact, everyone went armed during those days... I can truly say that George never saw a happy day after the tragedy. In 1871 he died of tuberculosis in a hospital at Galveston, about two and a half years after the death of John.... George Jackson was indicted for the offense, but the case was postponed from time to time and never came up for trial. Under the terms of Maj. Jackson's will his son John had been disinherited, but the will disappeared and was never probated.[144]

The death of John C. left the estate of Abner and Margaret Jackson without an administrator. Many petitions were submitted to the courts for the settlement of the estate. Wm. J. W. Masterson became executer of the estates of Abner and Margaret Jackson. After the death of John C. an attempt to hold the estate together was made, but documents indicate that debtors were demanding payment. The estate was sold piece by piece. The estate was finally settled in 1873.

George W. died of tuberculosis on November 7, 1871 in Galveston.[145] Of the Jackson children, only two remained: L. M. Stroble, son of Margaret Stroble Jackson, and Arsenath Jackson Groce, the wife of J. Fulton Groce and the daughter of Margaret and Abner Jackson. Arsenath's descendants are from her Granddaughters, Eva Lee Russell and Arsenath Jackson Wood. Frank Jackson, son of John C. and the Indian/African slave, Rose, is not mentioned in the probate records. There is no record that Frank received any portion of his father's estate. Frank had 14 children with many descendants residing in Brazoria County today.

---

[144] Stroble, Page 24
[145] Brazoria County Records: Will: 1871, Case No. 923

V.

Died in the AM, Buried in the PM: Slave Life in the Lower Brazos River Valley

On Thursday, July 16, 1863, the slave, Old Harvey, died about 8 A.M. on the Shrock Plantation. The slave, George, made the coffin and the slave, Presley, buried him in the afternoon.[1] Old Harvey was first mentioned in the plantation journal as being ill on July 2. He was mentioned as ill each day until his death. Old Harvey was not required to work in the fields in 1863. He is not listed with the other field hands in their daily activities. The only references to Old Harvey's activities in 1863 were on January 24, when he straightened the honey suckle, and on January 28, when he worked in the garden.

Slaves had little opportunity to tell their history, but from plantation journals, probate records, census records, newspapers, legal documents, and archaeological research, their lives in the Brazos region can be better understood. The slave quarters on the Lake Jackson Plantation were located either across the lake from the main plantation structures or on the banks of Oyster Creek. Both locations are covered by modern development prohibiting archaeological excavations.

Between the 1820s and the Civil War the Lower Brazos River Valley developed from a virgin land to a thriving populous of wealthy planters and farmers with slave labor and slave knowledge.

---

[1] Journal of Activities, H.G. Shrock Plantation, Wharton, County, Texas, 1860-1865

The slavery system of the South was similar in many ways to the feudal kingdoms of the middle ages. Abigail Curlee in her Ph.D. dissertation on Texas slave plantations in 1932, gives this description of plantation life in Texas.

> Plantation life had many compensations. If afforded a comfortable living; servants; leisure, even though not unmixed with vexations; a sense of importance; the satisfaction of being master over all one surveyed. Natural inertia hindered a man from withdrawing from the system, once he was in it. Its paternalism satisfied his vanity and in a measure compensated for his burdens and incessant annoyances. He was judge, law-giver, and ruler of his little world. His individualism, fettered by the accepted code of his day, knew little restraint other than that of his own conscience or of public opinion.[2]

Curlee also wrote that, "Negroes expected certain rights and privileges..."[3] They expected adequate food, clothing, housing, medical care, a certain number of hours of "private time" during a week, holidays and festivals, such as the end of the harvest season and Christmas, visitation rights to family and friends at nearby plantations, the right to own private possessions, and have their own money. It was in the planter's best interest to keep their Negroes as healthy and happy as possible. Planters paid little attention to what went on in the quarters. John B. Boles, in his 1984 book on the South, states, "But what slaves did in their cabins after sundown-- the tales they told, how they named and disciplined their children, the patterns in the baskets they wove, their characteristic gestures and loose, disjointed way of walking-- the master cared little

---

[2] Curlee, Abigail 1932, "A Study of Texas Slave Plantations, 1822-1865", PhD Dissertaion, University of Texas Department of History, Page 79.
[3] Curlee, 1932, Page IV

for such matters. And yet, here in the arena of the slave quarters, so much of what constituted the Afro-American was created."[4]

The plantation system of sugar and cotton depended on the labor and skills of the slave population. By the year 1860, in Brazoria County, slaves were more than 70% of the total population.[5]

Table 1.

Slave Populations In Brazoria County, Texas

Year	Total Population	White Population	Slave Population	Free Black Pop.
1840			1316	
1847	4641	1623 (34.97%)	3013 (64.92%)	5 (.01%)
1860	7155	2045 (28.58%)	5110 (71.42%)	?

With slaves outnumbering the free population by more than two to one, the control of the slave population became a concern during the Civil War. Abigail Curlee wrote that "... a Committee of Safety was organized in 1861 in Brazoria County at Columbia with John Adriance as Chairman. This Committee recommended that written passes, specifying the place and length of the visit be given Negroes leaving the master's premises; that Negroes be not permitted to attend any gathering more than five miles distant from the master's plantation; that Negroes be not allowed to trade during the holidays unless accompanied by a responsible person; that a Negro visiting his family more than five miles from home should have a written pass, stating the purpose, the time and the place of the visit."[6] Planters took turns patrolling at night to

---

[4] Boles, John B. Black Southerners 1619-1869, The University Press of Kentucky, 1984, Page 44
[5] Census Records for 1840, 1847, 1860
[6] Curlee, 1932 Page 131

discourage slaves from running away. This list of restrictions documents some of the privileges slaves had prior to 1861.

Slave owners called themselves planters when they owned 20 or more slaves. Many farmers and sons of planters called themselves "planters" because this status implied that they did not work in the fields side by side with their slaves as was the case with many small slave owners.

Table 2.

Slave Holders in Brazoria County in 1860, From The Slave Census Count

Number of Slave Owners, 158

Number of Planters, 67

# of slaves	1	2-4	5-9	10-19	20-49	50-99	100-199	200-299	300-400
slave owners	26	43	43	46					
planters					41	16	7	2	1

Table 3

Major Planters in Brazoria County in 1860[7]

300-400 Slaves Owned

Mills, David G., Robert, & Andrew	Lowood	192
	Bynum	120

---

[7] Slave Census of 1860

	Palo Alto	31 Total 343

200-300 Slaves Owned

Jackson, Abner	"Lake Place"	84
	Darrington	96
	Retrieve	105 Total 285
Bell, Josiah H.		213

100 - 200 Slaves Owned

McNeel, J. G.		176
Coffee, Aaron		157
Kennedy, William		144
Jordan, Levi		134
Wharton, J.A.		133
Mims, Alexander		103
Spencer, Joel		102

Slaves could be bought and sold freely in Texas especially in Houston and Galveston. Curlee, in her 1932 dissertation, gave this account of slave markets.

> In Houston were J. Castanie, A. R. Ruthven, an Englishman and licensed auctioneer, and Wynne and J. W. Wynne and R. B. Armfield; in Galveston, A. F. James whose agency had been established in 1842, Ira M. Freeman on Tremont Street, George H. Trabue on the Strand, and Ayres, Webb and Company of which David Ayres was a partner. Several firms kept slaves constantly on hand. In 1853, Thomas S. Gresham of Houston received direct from Virginia and Maryland a typical slave dealer's gang, consisting of 50 Negroes from ten to twenty five years old. Gresham announced that his prices

were as low as those in New Orleans. The next year R. A. Layton advertised his anxiety to sell 'fifty young likely Negroes' on Market Square. E. Riordan's slave depot, near the office of the Telegraph, was a land mark where Negroes were always on hand. In Galveston J. O. and H. M. Trueheart, Auctioneers, Land Locators, and General Agents, kept Negroes of all ages constantly on hand and for sale on commission. At the sign of the Red Flag on Market Street was the agency of C. L. McCarty, who not only sold slaves in the Galveston Slave Mart but also found employment for servants. In 1860, McMurry and Winstead at their depot in the Leonard building, back of the Tremont Hotel, offered thirty more choice Negroes, just arrived from Carolina and Virginia. This firm was receiving fresh lots every month.[8]

Curlee also noted that slaves were imported from Africa into Texas. "In 1840 Brazoria County had the doubtful distinction of receiving the last shipment of slaves to be brought to the shores of North America."[9] In 1975, James Creighton in a history of Brazoria County gave this account of one of the last slaves from Africa.

In a scrapbook which belonged to the late J. P. Underwood of East Columbia, dated around 1913, there is an interview with a slave named Ned Thompson who came in with this last shipment. At the time of the interview, he was living near Columbia, and, though he was more than ninety years old, his memory was clear as to all that had happened to him.

> He remembered well the battle in which his tribe had been defeated by a rival tribe and he had been taken prisoner, only to be sold by his captors to a slave trader. He remembered the trip over, first to Cuba and then straight to the mouth of the Bernard [River].
> "He has lived in this country eversince," Underwood wrote. "He remembers the customs and habits of the wild people of his native land. Speaks the language or dialect of his people fluently. He is an interesting man, dignified, polite, well preserved and happy."[10]

---

[8] Curlee, 1932, Page 50
[9] Creighton, James A., "A Narrative History of Brazoria County," Brazoria County Historical Commission, Printed by Texian Press, Waco, 1975, Page 171
[10] Ibid, Pages 173 and 174, Picture of Ned Thompson on Page 172.

Slaves not only had to produce market crops of sugar, cotton and corn, but they also had to produce the food eaten on the plantation, build the structures and roads, make their clothing; provide for the needs of the plantation. Before 1861, the planters built the roads. When plantations had common property lines, the planters would build the roads as a joint effort. The old road on the east side of the Brazos, from Velasco to Brazoria, was built and maintained by the slaves on the Herndon, Wharton and Jackson plantations, and kept in good condition. Many roads were ditched and corduroyed.[11]

Corn was the most important food crop produced in the Brazos River valley. Most farmers could grow two crops a year. The plantations and farmers with mills increased their profits by grinding corn meal for their neighbors. Between 1850 and 1860 farmers and planters while increasing their cotton production, produced about the same amount of corn per person, about 50 bushels.[12] Humans consumed about thirteen bushels of corn per person per year with the remaining used for livestock and as a cash crop. Crops such as wheat, oats, rye, peas, beans and potatoes provided another ten to twenty bushels per person. Slave holding farmers slaughtered livestock for home consumption, approximately two hogs per person per year.[13] Texas slaves usually had a diet that was adequate in calories and nutrition to promote good health.[14]

Healthy food was a primary concern for everyone on the plantation. Plantations varied in what and how slaves were fed. The two most common methods were to distribute food to slaves and allow them to cook their own, or to have a common kitchen where food was prepared for the slaves. Most large plantations preferred the common kitchen because it insured that the slaves

---

[11] Strobel, 1926, Page 55
[12] Campbell, 1989 Page 75
[13] Ibid
[14] Ibid, Page 147

were properly fed and allowed more time for the slaves to be in the field. Abigail Curlee Holbrook in her 1973 article included this account of food preparation.

> Mrs. Rosa Groce Bertleth described the magnitude of the food preparation at Groce's Bernardo plantation, with its hundred or so bondsmen. In order to have the workers in the fields by daylight, the call to arise came about 4 A.M. While the men were feeding the mules, the cooks were brewing pots of strong coffee. When the bell sounded at daylight, all the hands came to the dining hall for their "eye-opener" --- a cup of steaming coffee. All then went to the fields, the men to the ploughs and the women to the hoes. At 7 A.M. the breakfast, consisting of ham or bacon, hot biscuits or cornbread, and fresh steak or chicken, was packed in tin buckets and sent to the fields in carts for distribution to the workers. Dinner was cooked and served at 12 o'clock in the same manner. At 6 P.M. or sundown all gathered together at the hall for a hot meal.[15]

The former Texas slave, Thomas Cole's memories are recorded in the *Texas Narratives*. He remembered that there was always plenty of meat to eat. His master, Cole, saw that everyone got their share of meat and lard. Once a week all of the slaves had biscuits. There was an orchard of peaches and apples and the slaves had all the fruit they wanted. The slaves planted pumpkins and had pumpkin pies. They also had about two acres planted in watermelon that the slaves worked on Saturday evening. He remembered plenty of vegetables to eat and [Coles stated] "if anyone went without them, it was their own fault."[16]

To produce cane, cotton, and corn and perform all the yearly plantation task required tremendous labor and numerous technological skills. Plantation journals and other documents

---

[15] Abigail Curlee Holbrook, "A Glimpse of Life on Antebellum Slave Plantations, *Southwestern Historical Quarterly*, The Texas State Historical Association, Vol. LXXVI, No. 4, April, 1973 pp. 370

[16] Silverthorne, Elizabeth, Plantation Life in Texas, Texas A & M University Press: College Station, 1986, pp. 95. From *Texas Narratives*, pp. 788-789

record the slave's work schedules for the year.[17] By carefully examining these various duties, we can understand the skills and knowledge required by the slaves. The yearly work schedule is in the Appendices.

In 1860, at the Lake Jackson Plantation, there were 84 slaves.

Table 4

Slaves By Age and Sex at Lake Jackson

Ages	0-5	6-10	11-15	16-20	21-30	31-40	41-50
Males	15	3	2	4	14	7	3
Females	8	3	3	2	13	5	1

Lowe and Campbell, through their research, make the assumption that in Texas, children under ten did no field work; children between 10 and 14 did half as much field work as an adult; males between 15 and 49 could do a full days work in the field; females between 15 and 49 could do two thirds as much work as male field hands.[18] By this method of calculation we would subtract the 29 children under the age of 11 from the work force. Also subtracted from the field count would be the women, about 5, who prepared the meals for the main house and slaves; cleaned in the main house; cared for the young children and made the clothing. Slaves listed by name and duty for the Jackson Plantation were: Major, age 45, who was a driver, a slave overseer in the fields; Andrew, age 40, was listed as a carpenter; Peter, age 40, a blacksmith; Black

---

[17] H.G. Shrock's Plantation Journal of Activities, Wharton County, Recorded between 1860 and 1865; Abner and Margaret Jackson Probate Records; Elizabeth Silverthorne's Plantation Life in Texas; J. Carlyle Sitterson, *Sugar Country: The Cane Sugar Industry in the South, 1763-1960;*1953 University of Kentucky Press, Page 112

[18] Lowe, Richard G. and Randolph B. Campbell, Planters & Plain Folk: Agriculture in Antebellum Texas, Southern Methodist University Press, Dallas, 1987, pp.161

Abram, age 30, a cooper; Big William, age 37, an engineer; and Ned, age 42, also listed as a cooper. At various times Andrew, Peter, Black Abram, Big William and Ned would not be available for field work but would be busy with their own tasks. This means that the 45-50 field hands at the Jackson Plantation, were responsible for 500-600 acres of sugar cane, 200-300 acres of cotton, 50 acres of corn, 500 head of cattle, 100 hogs, the other plantation animals, and all of the plantation tasks.

In Randolph B. Cambell's *An Empire for Slavery: THE PECULIAR INSTITUTION IN TEXAS*, he summarizes the labors of Texas slaves.

> A minority of the slaves who lived on farms and plantations were not field workers, at least not primarily. Instead, they spend most of their time at other jobs, many of which required special training and skills. Men worked as blacksmiths, carpenters, brick masons, coopers, cobblers, tanners, and in the general repair of farm implements and machinery. The proportion of such workers among Texas agricultural slaves cannot be determined with any precision, but it appears that most owners of ten or more bondsmen had at least a few engaged largely in non field labor.[19] ... the majority of Texas slaves worked on farms and plantations. Men, women, and children shared, as their physical capabilities permitted, in clearing and improving land, cultivating field crops and gardens, tending livestock, and performing necessary chores. Inclement weather and slack seasons undoubtedly gave some relief from labor, as did the common practice of allowing bondsmen to have Saturday afternoons and Sundays as free time; nevertheless, long hours of hard and monotonous work were the rule. A sizable minority of slaves, perhaps 10 to 20 percent of the total, served as skilled hands or house servants or lived in towns. They enjoyed an advantage over field hands

---

[19] Cambell, Randolph B., *An Empire for Slavery: The Peculiar Institution In Texas*, 1989, pp. 122

in that their work generally was less physically burdensome, but in many cases they probably worked longer hours under closer supervision by whites. Some Texas bondsmen held positions of responsibility, and a few were even able to take the initiative in determining the work that they did. Many had the opportunity to earn at least a little money of their own. Unremitting labor and the acceptance of responsibility, however, did not necessarily earn satisfactory material conditions and decent physical treatment for all Texas slaves.[20]

Young children may not have worked in the field, but they played a part in the work force. Children seven, eight and nine, often helped care for the younger children, helped distribute meals and water to the field hands, gathered eggs, churned butter, weeded the garden and performed countless other task around the plantation. Very young children even contributed through play. "Husking peas was a favorite task for the black children because after the peas were put in sacks, the children would stomp barefooted on them until the hulls broke away from the peas. Then, on a windy day, the contents of the sacks were winnowed like wheat until the hulls had blown away."[21]

Sugar production is very labor intensive task for the adults. During the sugar boiling season, everyone helped in the process. Another labor intensive factor in sugar production is the fuel required to boil down the sugar syrup in the reduction process. Between 3-5 cords of wood[22] were used for each hogshead. Using the recorded number of hogsheads and barrels of molasses produced for the Jackson Plantation, the containers and wood needed can be estimated.

---

[20] Ibid, pp. 132
[21] Silverthorne, 1986, pp.89
[22] A cord is a measurement of cut wood equal to 128 cubic feet. A pile of wood 4 feet high, 4 feet wide, and 8 feet long is a cord.

Table 5

Lake Jackson Plantation Sugar Production[23]

Year	Hogsheads	Molasses	Barrels Needed	Cords of Wood
1852	296	888	1184	1500
1853	142	426	568	750
1854	160	480	640	800
1855	133	399	532	565
1856	0			
1857	0			
1858	90	270	360	450

Cotton was also a labor intensive crop. The 200-300 acres for cotton at the Jackson Plantation were prepared in January and February. Planting was in March, and the harvest would begin in July. The ginning and baling could last through the winter.

Another way to look at the skills required of slaves working on the plantations is to look at the skills listed in the 1860 census records for Brazoria County; plantation owners who did not own slaves with specific skills and small farmers would hire free laborers for specific tasks. The occupations of the people in any county during any census will reveal the skills, and professions needed to support the economic processes in the county.

Clothing was another time consuming task on the plantations. Usually, slaves received two sets of clothing per year; one for summer and one for winter. Some plantations wove their own cloth but most bought yardage. "Planters calculated that the labor of a woman in the field could buy many more yards of cloth than she could spin and weave in the same time. By the bolt,

---

[23] In 1856 and 1857, frost and heavy rains ruined the sugar crops in Brazoria county.

planters bought osnaburg,[24] jeans, kersey, lowells, and linsey-woolsey."[25] The sewing of the garments was done by the mistress of the plantation and/or the overseer's wife, with help from the slaves. "Of these coarse garments each man was issued in the spring two pairs of pants, two shirts, and a straw hat; in the fall, two more pairs of pants (usually of a heavier material), two shirts, a coat, and a woolen hat. Twice a year, also, the women donned new dresses and "linens."[26] Much time was required to make garments for large numbers of slaves. Slaves might receive their clothing piece by piece over two to three months.[27] Slave garments were very functional and sometimes of poor quality. "General James Hamilton [half owner of Retrieve Plantation with Abner Jackson] was shocked at the scanty clothing furnished the hired slaves on the Retrieve Plantation in Brazoria County by Major Abner Jackson. 'In this dreadful cold weather, they have received a flimsy Negro cloth & a scanty patter at that.' Four days later the general was modifying his several charges against Jackson. By then he understood that the Negroes 'were about as well clothed as the average of Plantation in the Country were.' The clothing did not compare with that worn by slaves in South Carolina and Mississippi with which Hamilton was familiar. He planned to give the Negroes a suit around before he left."[28]

Saturday afternoons were usually set aside for the cleaning of houses, persons, and clothing. "...lye soap was plentiful and was much used, though needles and thread were treasures."[29] Slave housing varied from plantation to plantation. "Usually the cabin for a slave family was a one room building, about 20' X 20', with a fireplace for cooking and heating. A

---

[24] A kind of coarse, heavy linen or cotton used for furnishings and sacks.
[25] Holbrook, 1973, pp. 370
[26] Ibid, pp. 373
[27] Ibid
[28] Ibid, pp. 374
[29] Ibid, pp. 375

loft, reached by a ladder built against a wall, was the sleeping room for the boys if the family was a large one."[30] "Because of the insects and for other sanitary reasons, slave owners usually insisted that slave houses be scalded or scrubbed often and that bedding be aired. Regular cleaning of the cabins was the rule not the exception on Texas plantations."[31] The slave quarters at the Lake Jackson Plantation were either across the lake from the main house or near Brazoria Creek. Structure B near the main house may have been occupied by house servants. Some of the artifacts are not what one would expect to find in slave quarters. It may be that the Jackson family lived in structure B while the main house was being built, and it was then occupied by the house servants. The interior walls were white washed, a common practice on plantations. Much of the lime the planters purchased was used to whitewash Negro homes and other outbuildings."[32]

The health of slaves and family was of great concern to planters. Doctors were frequently called to care for the ill or injured. During the year of 1860, Dr. John M. Prewitt visited the Lake Jackson Plantation 36 times to care for Negroes, servants and horses.[33] On January 1, 1862, Dr. Prewitt presented his bill of $27. 25 for his services between January 2, 1861 and December 25th, 1861. On January 2, 1861 he attended Caesar, a slave. On September 4, he attended the youngest son, and again on September 25. This might be a reference to Abner Jackson Jr.[34]

On December 11, 1862 a bill was presented for services in 1862. On March 8, the Dr. found a tumor in the leg of the Negro woman, Abbey; on March 24, the leg was amputated; the

---

[30] Ibid, pp. 362
[31] Ibid, pp. 362
[32] Ibid, pp. 367
[33] Jackson Probate Records, File 4, Item 180
[34] Ibid, File 4, Item 74

Dr. made 16 visits to Abbey to dress the stump. Abbey is listed in the probate records as being 33 and with one leg. On July 10, he visited Cely at daylight and attended her until 2 P.M. when she died. The cost for these visits was $325.[35] A bill was also presented by a Dr. Gowring on December of 1862, for 14 visits between $3-$5 per visit. The total was $50.[36] At the Darrington Plantation in 1863, the Dr.'s charges were $417.[37] Also during 1863, a Dr. P.P. McRue attended the slave, Caldwell, who had received a gun shot wound. Between September 9, and October 28, the Dr. visited Caldwell thirteen times and charged $191.[38] On May 8, 1863 one bottle of quinine was purchased for the Lake Jackson Plantation for a cost of $25.[39] "The Negroes seemed to be peculiarly susceptible to pneumonia. Remedies were herbs, teas, brews, quinine, calomel, blue mass, Epson salts, mustard, castor oil, aloes, and cupping."[40] On May 3, 1865, John C. Jackson purchased from George and Davidson Druggist in Houston, 1 gallon of castor oil for $2.50, 1 gallon of calomel for $2.50, 1 gallon of blue mass for $2.00 and 1/2 gallon of alpaca.[41] Dr. Theophilus Field charged $420 to the Jackson Estate for his medical services in 1865.[42] Planters feared most infectious diseases that could spread between plantations. "Of all diseases, the planters dreaded most yellow fever and cholera. During epidemics slaves who worked in the field one day could be dead the next morning. In 1833 cholera hit the area between the Brazos and Colorado rivers with dreadful results. Again in 1847 cholera struck and

---

[35] Ibid, File 6, Item 286
[36] Ibid, File 6, Item 55
[37] Ibid, File 6, Item 6
[38] Ibid, File 6, Item 9
[39] Ibid, File 6, Item 67
[40] Holbrook, pp. 376. "cupping" -A medical bleed by using a glass in which a partial vacuum is formed by heating.
[41] Jackson Probate Records, File 6, Item 206
[42] Ibid, File 6, Item 8

the planters scattered their hands in the woods and suspended all work...Abner Jackson lost nine."[43] Another contagious disease of great concern was measles. On April 15, 1864, John C. Jackson bought a gallon of liquor for $15.75 from L. P. Bingham "for Negroes during measles."[44]

The planters were also attentive to the religious education of their slaves. On January 1, 1862 a payment of $40 was made to Thomas H. Hindson for his missionary labor among his Negroes on the Darrington plantation for the year 1860. He also received $100 for his missionary labors on the Darrington, Lake Jackson and Retrieve plantations for the year 1861.[45] "Slaves avidly accepted Christianity and made it their own because it served their purposes so well. As the white ministers often said the Bible proclaimed, slaves understood that in the eyes of God all men are equal, bondservant and free alike."[46] Some records suggests that the Jacksons were harder on their slaves than most planters. Lake Jackson Negroes worked more hours than most slaves. Tom Jenkins, a former Jackson slave, told Walter Crosby of Gulf Prairie that on Sunday mornings the Negroes arose early and worked as usual until 9:00 o'clock. Then the observance of the Sabbath began. Most slave owners gave Negroes all day Sunday.

Slaves were treated differently on each plantation, some used the whip and others did not. "Some Negroes were so hardened to the lash that it affected nothing. The "Lake Jackson" and Patton Negroes in Brazoria County bore a bad reputation and neighboring planters thought they required a heavy hand."[47] Slaves developed their own ways of coping with the dehumanizing

---

[43] Holbrook, pp. 376
[44] Jackson Probate Records, File 4, Item 252
[45] Ibid, File 4, Item 139
[46] Boles, 1984, pp. 157
[47] Curlee, 1932, pp. 122

environment of slavery. John Boles in his book on Southern slavery gave this description of slave behavior.

> Fully aware of their situation, they learned, socialized, and passed on to their children a wide range of behavior-- voice intonations, facial expressions, feigned illness, purposeful laziness and slowness of motion, dumb-like-a-fox incomprehension-- that combined equal portions of insubordination and minor rebellion to produce a constant undercurrent of resistance to psychological bondage. Although never completely giving in to authority, most slaves were able, at least in the eyes of their master, to acquiesce in their state of servitude and thus survive with their essential humanity intact.[48]

http://web.mac.com/joan_few

---

[48] Boles, 1984, Page 175

VI.

Juneteenth and Beyond

On the nineteenth of June in 1865, General Gordon Granger of the United States Army in Galveston, Texas, proclaimed that slaves in Texas were free; Juneteenth. This day became a day of celebration for the freedmen and ... "no Negro was expected to show up for work on that day."[1]

Newly freed slaves could leave their former masters. Some did, and others remained to become wage earners. John C. Jackson, on the Darrington Plantation, began "paying" his freed slaves in July of 1865. They did not receive their wages until December 24, 1865. Before they received payment, any fines, loans or charges at the plantation store were deducted.

Scattered throughout the 900 documents in Abner and Margaret Jackson's probate records are small individual receipts, lists of names, payments, and financial records that document how the "Black hands," at the Darrington plantation were paid by John Jackson, executor of the Jackson estate.

Southern planters, "accepted with resentment that freedmen now had to be paid wages, but landowners expected blacks to dwell once more in the former slave quarters bunched together near the big house and to work the fields in gangs under close white supervision. Sometimes wages were paid monthly in cash (about $10 per month for an adult male), but usually half the wages were payable at the end of the year after the crops were harvested."[2]

---

[1] Creighton, 1975, pp. 258
[2] Boles, 1984, pp. 207

Laborers on the Darrington Plantation were paid different daily wages according to their tasks and abilities. They were also paid different wages during different work periods. Wages were lower in July, August, and September, higher for October and November when sugar was being harvested and the sugar mill was in operation, then lower wages for December. Darrington plantation workers were provided with housing, and food on the days they worked. We are assuming that they lived in the slave quarters and food was provided as it had been under the slavery system. If workers did not work, they were charged board for that day at a rate higher than they would receive for working. Board was 50¢ most days and $1.17 a day during sugar making season.

Wages[3] For A Days Labor Between July and December, 1865

Darrington Plantation, Texas

Names: Wages per day for:

	July - Sept.	Oct.-Nov.	Dec.
Sophia & Venea	7.6¢	15.2¢	7.6¢
Judy	15¢	16¢	15¢
Elcy and Joe Mack	15¢	30¢	15¢
Hicks & Dennis	19¢	38¢	19¢
Tony, Eady, Daphne	23¢	46¢	23¢
Pallas	23¢	46¢	23¢
Lucinda & Parthenia	25¢	50¢	25¢
Mary, Sarah, Sarah Lake	27¢	54¢	27¢
Santa Anna (Santanna ?)	27¢	54¢	27¢
Little Andrew	27¢	54¢	27¢

[3] Wages are listed on individual receipts in the Jackson Probate Records, File 6, all of the receipts are hand written and many are hard to read. Questionable spellings of names are indicated.

Big Ellen	27¢	54¢	27¢
Angeline & Travis	30.7¢	61.5¢	30.7¢
Molly & Maria	30.7¢	61.5¢	30.7¢
Mandy, Debby, & Nancy	30.7¢	61.5¢	30.7¢
Bill Jack	37.2¢	78.4¢	37.2¢
Pate	38¢	76¢	38¢
Henry, Hiram, Sam Johnson	39.2¢	78.4¢	39.2¢
Armstead Green, Walton, Big Jim, and Wash	39.2¢	78.4¢	39.2¢
Moses	39.2¢	$1.15	38.5¢

Some workers were paid just by the day or month: Old Annub, 19¢ per day; Old Salvive, 15¢; Old Harry, 39¢; Lea, 15¢ (increased to 19¢); Caldwell, 30.7¢ with a yearly total of $61.50; January, $6 per month and $3 per month; Scott and Sando, $20 a month; Jim Doto, 7 days for $4.75; Mavey Ann, 61¢; Charles Terry, 27¢; Shadrack, $10 per month; Big William worked for 96 days at 39.2¢ per day for a total of $37 and 63.2¢; Fork, 13 days for $3; Peter, 13 days for $10; New Moses for $10 a month; Sam Willis for $30 a month; Jim Ray, 30 days at the sugar mill for $23.15; Patsy, 150 days at 23¢ per day; and Big Andrew, 150 days for $173.07.

Individuals with special skills were paid by the job. The bricklayer, Bob, was paid $30 for a month's work at Darrington. Bob was listed as a slave at Lake Jackson and was about 42 years old.

Lake Bob [or Bob Lake] was paid $20 for one month of labor in the sugar mill. On October 3, 1865, he was paid $15 for sharpening the gin at Darrington.

When June 19, 1866 came, it was considered by the former slaves as a day of independence, a day for celebration and was allowed, as a holiday, by most employers in Texas.

John Jackson would not allow a free day to celebrate Juneteenth and docked his workers $5 for not working on the "Teenth." This was the equivalent, for most workers, of two weeks or more of wages.

In 1866, there was a slight difference from 1865, in the way wages were calculated at the Darrington Plantation. Laborers were given receipts of payment on November 1, 1866. These receipts listed their names (which now include surnames), the amount of work, the number of days of work, and their wages. It also included the amounts for which they were docked and frequently the reason for the monetary fine. They were charged 50¢ a day for room and board if they did not work, which was more than most earned in a day.

Daphney (or Daphine) Jackson worked for 30¢ a day, picked 740 lbs of cotton at 50¢ per 100 pounds, and worked 17 days and 6 nights in the sugar mill (sugar rolling) for $6.90. She was docked $5 for refusing to work on Juneteenth, and 50¢ per day for 85 days for board. Daphney was about 30 years old and had been a slave on the Jackson plantation.

William Fields worked for 50¢ a day and worked 21 days and 9 nights in the sugar mill.

Abram Day worked from January 3, 1866 to October at $15 a month. He made 60 hogsheads barrels at $1 each. He spent 23 days repairing hogsheads and kegs and split 550 rails at 75¢ a hundred. On December 31, an additional receipt lists 60 hogsheads made, 6 sugar buckets repaired, 136 barrels and 12 hogsheads repaired. Abram Day is probably the slave, Black Abram, who was the cooper on the Jackson plantation. He was about 34.

Francis Gibbons worked for 50¢ a day, picked 668 lbs of cotton, and worked 19 days and 9 nights in the sugar mill. Deducted from his wages was $3 for schooling and $40 for a horse.

Wesi (or Wise) Woods worked for 159 days at 50¢ a day and worked 19 days and 10 nights in the sugar mill. His total was $94. Deducted from his wages was $30 cash, a coat at $8.50, rails at $15, board fine of $1.50, and $75 for a horse. This left him $41 in debt. There was a slave named Wise on the Darrington plantation; he would have been about 26.

Monday Small worked for 112 and 1/2 days at 40¢ per day, picked 489 pounds of cotton at 50¢ per pound and worked 12 days and 7 nights in the sugar mill. His total was $57.84. He was charged $5.50 for board, docked $10, $2.50 for groceries, $1.50 for school, docked $5 for riding the horse Jeff Davis, and he purchased a mare for $30. He received $3.34 in payment.

Solomon Maclin worked 173 days at $2.50 a day for $432.50. He also made 4 pair of hinges and 3 pairs of springs for $2.20. Deducted was $58 for 1800 feet of lumber, $4 for shingles, and $2 for planes. He also purchased groceries and cement for a total amount of $324.54. His balance was $110.16.

Hiram Mitchell (or Mitchel) worked 177 and 1/2 days at 50¢ a day and worked 21 days in the sugar mill. Deducted from his wages was $52.50 for a cash loan, $16.95 for items bought at the store, and $4.50 for schooling.

Sarah Mitchell worked for 171 and 1/2 days at 30¢ per day and picked 884 pounds of cotton at 50¢ per hundred pound. Deducted from her wages was $3 for a cash loan.

Henry Barry worked 111 days at 30¢ per day and worked 21 days and 9 nights in the sugar mill. Deducted from his wages was $12 for a cash advance, $5.15 for groceries, $1.50 for board, $3 for shoes and $14.10 for his store account.

Myers Brown (or Browns) worked for 73 days at 40¢ a day and he worked 14 days and 10 nights in the sugar mill. He was docked $25 for breaking a gate, $15 for neglect of duty and $3 for a doctor bill.

Also listed with receipts were Abram Ferrel (or Fend), Walton Payne, Louisa Austin, Samuel Johnson, Washington Payne, Dan Woods, Santanna, Lizzie Small, (Black) Robert Strobel, Amanda, Isabella Small, Moses Bowling, Aaron Bowling, Sam Cohn, Andrew Payne, Solomon, Linda Day, Indgin (or Ingin) James, Abram Mills, Dennis Green, Lolie Smith, Julia Jackson, Lucinda Hutchins, Frances Mitchell (also docked $5 for refusing to work on Juneteenth), Joseph Mack, Liddie Parkson, Debby McNeil, Becky Taylor, Maria Mitchell, Betty Ray, Julia Mills, Charles Jackson, Mo Hutchins, Rufus White, Douglas Winters, Duncan Jackson, Thomas Jenkins (docked $5 for using a mule at night), William Payne, Samuel Luckis (sp?); Moses James, Jake Jackson, Honey Love, Hamp, Shadrack Jackson, Pat Mitchell, Jim Mitchell, Washington Gibbs, Charlotte Johnson, Sam Jiles, John, Tom Austin, Eson, Frederick, Borrell, Becky L., Ohio McNeil, Ellen Green, Julia Bringham, Ernest Daniel, Chaney Mitchell, Halston Knight, Mary Payson (or Paysen), Thomas Austin, and Amanda Austin.

A list of payment to "black hands" has no date but is probably for the year 1866 or later. The hands are listed in family groups and there was no itemization of their amount of labor or items for which they were docked or charged against their account. Names in Bold correspond to names on slave lists either at the Jackson or Darrington plantations.

List of payment to "black hands" [4]

Amanda Austin	85.80
Thomas Austin	70.85
Louisa Austin	68.65
Julia Bingham	50.17
Moses Bolen	22.50
Aaron Bolen	22.50
Myers Brown	38.80
Henry Buzzey (sp. ?)	42.30
Samuel Colier	22.50
Jim Davis	16.00
Abram Day	252.62
Juda Day	83.20
Earnest Daniels	53.87
Andrew DeCosta	315.00
Francis Gibbons	97.34
Washington Gibbs	15.20
Algerago Goffang	349.00
Amanda Gooseberry	13.83
Nancy Gordon	81.34
Santana Gordon	87.68
(a Santa Anna, age 15, in Lake Jackson Inventory)	
Ellen Green	108.36
(Little Ellen, age 25, in Darrington Inventory)	
Also a Big Ellen, age 48, listed - Mother?	
Joe Green	110.91
(age, 28, Darrington Inventory)	
Dennis Green	81.90
(age 12, in Darrington Inventory)	
Abram Ferrel	119.65
William Fields	58.50
Daphne Jackson	51.40
Samuel Jackson	86.50

---

[4] Jackson Probate Records, File 6, Item 156

Jake Jackson	90.60
(age 52, Lake Jackson Inventory)	
Shadrack Jackson	101.37
Lydia Jackson	67.20
(age 25, Lake Jackson Inventory)	
Daufney Jackson	46.30
(age 26, lake Jackson Inventory)	
Angie James	97.44
Moses James	121.75
Dolly Jenkins	56.34
Thomas Jenkins	113.50
Charlotte Johnson	65.14
Holston Knight	222.81
Toney Love	18.80
Joseph Mack	64.65
Solomon Maclin	?
Ohio McNeel	133.25
Debby McNeel	69.59
Abram Mills	14.50
Dan Mills	101.50
Jim Mitchel	111.28

(Jim Mitchel was listed by first and last name in the July 1, 1862 inventory of the estate of Abner and Margaret Jackson, as a slave on the Darrington Plantation, age 29.)

Rhoda Mitchel	56.45

(A Rhoda, age 25, was listed on the Darrington inventory and could be a sister of Jim.)

Sarah Mitchel	55.87

(A Sarah, age 19, was listed on the Darrington inventory and could be a sister of Jim.)

Frances Mitchel	78.94

(A Francis, age 20, was listed on the Darrington inventory and could be a sister of Jim.)

Hiram Mitchel	109.75

(A Hiram, age 40 and a Hiram, age 6, were listed on the Darrington inventory and could be relatives of Jim.)

Pete Mitchel	107.00
(A Pete, age 26, is listed on the Darrington inventory.)	
Maria Mitchel	99.97
(A Maria, age 39, is listed on the Darrington inventory)	
Chaney Mitchel	57.67
(A Chaney, age 15, is listed on the Darrington inventory)	
William Navigan	91.20
Andrew Paine (Payne?)	96.00
Washington Payne	123.61
William Payne	123.00
Mary Payne	84.84
Walton Payne	122.00
Monday Pinkney	107.33
Sancho Robertson	126.17
Isabella Small	43.40
Monday Small	57.84
Lizzie Small	52.33
Felix Smith	86.86
(Black) Robert Strobel	131.50
Becky Taylor	62.20
Samuel Tucker	120.87
Rufus White	56.00
Samuel Willis	330.00
Wise Woods	94.00
(A Wise on Darrington Inventory)	
Hamp Wood	76.80
Don Wood Jr.	70.30
Dan Woods	45.66

The appearance on this document of family groupings supports the desire of black families to solidify their family units by last names and legal marriages. In the Confederate States conquered by Union troops, before the end of the war, this family bonding began immediately. "The strength of the freedmen's desire to cement their marriages - legally nonexistent and in practice often fragile during slavery - revealed itself as thousands of black couples came to Union army chaplains to have their vows solemnized."[5]

A separate list gives amounts received from Negroes "on account of things furnished them off plantation and for board while unemployed and for fines for misconduct and abuse of team and tools during year 1866."[6] (The complete list is in the Appendices.) Total collected was $949.94.

On May 3, 1867, John C. Jackson paid bonuses to "Negroes" for exception work.[7] To:

Hard Times	$10
(Hard Times was a slave on the Jackson plantation and about 46.)	
Poldo	$10
Jeff	$35
Dolley	$45
Hannah	$45
Charlotte	$30
Betsy	$30
(was a slave on Jackson plantation and about 16)	
Sugar	$23
(was a slave on Jackson plantation and about 15)	
Leffee	$10
Scott	$10
Mary Ann	$7

These bonuses totaled $250.

John Jackson also gave a bonus of $150 to Peter. Peter was listed as a blacksmith on the Lake Jackson slave rolls and was about 44 years old. Jackson served as a banker to his workers. When a person borrowed money from Jackson, they were given a note and their names were written out. They signed their "X" mark by their names or between the first and last names.

---

[5] Boles, 1984, pp. 200
[6] Jackson Probates, Folder 6, Item 320
[7] Ibid, Item 326

August 5, 1866	$11 to F.R. Rightmen at 2% interest
	$15 to Santana Gordon
January 8, 1867	Jim Mitchell $25
	Pete Mitchel $12
January 9, 1867	Dan Woods $9.
January 10, 1867	Washington Love $1
January 15, 1867	Dan Woods $11.70
January 19, 1867,	Philip Bolding $4.50

John Jackson also ran a plantation store at Darrington. Some of the items purchased were:

Pinkey	shoes	$2.25
Little Rhoda	1 pr. gloves	$1.75
Red Abraham	calico	40¢ a yard
Sarah	shirt	$1
Sarah Lake	candy	
Sophia	silk scarf	
Santanna	thimble	20¢

On December 4, 1867, John C. Jackson was killed by his brother, George. Just prior to his death, there are two records of payments to workers on December 1. Laura Jackson was paid $23.20 for 58 days of work and Caldwell Jackson was paid $32 for 64 days of work, and he was docked $14.

L. M. Strobel, the son of Margaret Jackson's first marriage, and Thomas W. Masterson became executers of the estate of Margaret and Abner Jackson. Their probate records do not list agreements or wages for plantation workers.

In the cotton South, the wage earning system gave way to the sharecrop system. "No matter how much had changed, the whites still owned the land, still controlled the government, and the blacks had only their labor to offer. As it turned out, whites needed black labor as badly as blacks needed white-owned land, and gradually, as in the days of slavery, by push and shove, give and take, mutual accommodations were worked out that resulted generally in a system of agriculture called sharecropping."[8] This system, of allowing laborers to use land in exchange for a share of the crop, worked for cotton, but it did not work for sugar. You can divide the cane fields but the sugar mill could not be divided. Producing sugar required a large cooperative labor force for an intense period of harvesting and refining. To secure this labor force, Texas sugar planters turned to renting convict laborers from the Texas Prison System.

http://web.mac.com/joan_few

---

[8] Boles, 1984, pp.199

VII

The Convict Lease System In Texas
And
Convicts at Lake Jackson Plantation

Texas built its first prison in Huntsville in 1849 for three prisoners. By 1860, the prison population had grown to 182. Cotton and wool mills were installed in the prison in the 1850s and prisoners were making money for the state weaving cotton and wool. They could process 500 bales of cotton and 6,000 pounds of wool annually.[1] Most of this cloth was sold to planters for slave clothing.

After the Civil War the prison had difficulty in getting raw materials and selling their cloth.[2] Also, the prison population was increasing. In 1867, 150 state prisoners were contracted to the Brazos Branch Railroad at $12.50 per month per man. This contract lasted only a few months because too many prisoners escaped or were killed or wounded in attempted escapes. In 1869, Texas had over 400 prisoners.[3] In 1871, the state leased the Huntsville State Prison and all the prisoners to Ward, Dewey & Co. of Galveston for a 15 year period. The prison conditions improved during the first few years of this lease and then begin to decline.[4]

The Lake Jackson Plantation began leasing convicts about 1873. That year William Walter Phelps bought the plantation from the estate of George W. Jackson and his sister, Mrs. Groce for $20,800. He sold it that same year to A.J. Ward and E.D. Deevey for $36,000.

---

[1] Walker, Donald R. 1988 *Penology For Profit: A History of the Texas Prison System, 1867 - 1912,* Texas A & M University Press, College Station, Page 16
[2] Ibid, Page 17
[3] Ibid, Pages 21-22
[4] Ibid

As part of the convict lease system, the State of Texas required that inspections be made of the locations and conditions of the convicts. In 1874, the inspector of the Lake Jackson convicts was a Mr. J.K.P. Campbell. He reported,

> At Lake Jackson plantation, in September, 1874, I found sixty five sick convicts confined in the prison out of a force of one hundred and eighty-five, some of whom were quite sick. These men at the time had no medical attention. There was a hospital steward on the place who had some knowledge of medicine, coupled with some experience as a nurse, but he was very ill himself, and unable to give any attention to the sick. I at once made the sergeant send for a physician who visited the camp the next day. He found the most essential medicines were not at the camp, and the sergeant had to send to Houston for them. In the meantime the men were without the medicine which had been prescribed. The physician expressed as his belief that two or three of the men were beyond the reach of medicine. The sick occupied the same building with the well convicts, and the attention required of the sick prevented the other men from obtaining that sleep which laboring men need.[5]

On pages 15 and 20 of the same report, the following was recorded.

> At the Lake Jackson Plantation, which I visited in September, 1874, I found three trusty convicts whose backs were cut to pieces in a most shocking manner. The only offense, so far as I could learn, committed by these *brutally treated men,* was, they had taken some flour and exchanged it for whisky, and returned to camp intoxicated.
>
> ...... From all I can learn the planters, with three or four exceptions, have fed their forces very well: but on plantations cultivated by the lessees, there

---

[5] 1874-1876 *Report on the Condition of the Texas State Penitentiary,* Page 13. Contained in, Report of The Board of directors of The Texas State Penitentiary, To The Governor, March 1876, A.C. Gray, State Printer, Houston

has been some complaint of short rations. At Lake Jackson, the sergeant informed me, that, at times, he was short of meat. He had to pledge his own credit to procure beef.

...... At the Lake Jackson plantation the sergeant, who has been on that place for sixteen months, informed me the convicts had not changed their clothing for ten weeks, and that the lower extremities of some of them were naked. The Assistant Inspector reports this camp badly in need of clothing. He also reported that the night he left, some clothing was put off at the landing for this camp. The camps are not well supplied with bedding, and in some instances, the men had to sleep on the mattress without cover.

This later report[6] was made (though dated August 31, 1874) *after* his [Inspector Campbell] September visit, where he says speaking of Lake Jackson and other camps, "There is no observable difference between them (the convicts) and free men engaged in the same kind of labor, except that the convict seems better clothed, fed, and in better health." On his return to Huntsville from his September visit to Lake Jackson, he reported to the Board of Directors the condition of that plantation as *entirely satisfactory,* and commended its management as being particularly good in every respect.

In December, 1876, when Inspector J. T. Gaines made his rounds, two tragic incidents had occurred at Lake Jackson. His report reads,

Huntsville, Texas, December 20, 1876
Lake Jackson, Sergeant Shaw
9th of December

---

[6] *Report of the Lessees of the Texas State Penitentiary, April, 1876*

No. in ranks 37. <u>do</u> [duty] Trustees 22, died 3. Total number 62

Day guards 7, Night <u>do</u> [duty]2

#5352 Frank Furlow died in stocks, a written report of which accompanies this report.

#5359 Wiley Wilson convict was killed on the 9th mist [sic] while attempting to make his escape by C.E. Whitten, guard, on an investigation of this killing I formed the same facts as stated in the accompanying written statement to ? [unreadable word in original manuscript]. The convict had got in the standing cane some distance when he was shot.

5312 Jas Taylor died Nov. 1 from natural causes.

Men are fed well. Prison in good order and but for these two unfortunate circumstances this camp is doing well.

In the *Report of the Inspector of the Texas State Penitentiary, Located at Huntsville, Texas, To the Governor of Texas,* (1876) Frank Furlow is listed on page 21 as convict #535. He was a black male, seventeen years of age from Anderson County who was convicted of theft of mare and mule and sentenced to 10 years. He was received in Huntsville on June 22, 1876. No records could be found on when he arrived at Lake Jackson.

Wiley Wilson, #542, is also listed on page 21 along with Frank Furlow in the 1876 report. Wiley was 15 years old, was born in South Carolina; was convicted of theft in Harris County and was sentenced to two years.

The official report of the Frank Furlow death is in the Individual Reports of the Texas State Penitentiary System in the Texas State Archives.

I have the honor to hand you my official report from the Lake Jackson farm in Brazoria County, Texas, managed and owned by Mr. Ward Duvey [Mr. A.

J. Ward and Mr. E. D. Deevey]. This in the matter of stocking one convict Frank Furlow on the 27th day of November, 1876.

I was on said farm December 9th 1876 when I investigated the said stocking and found that Sergeant Shaw had been absent on that day and had left a squad of men in charge of Guard Sumner with permission to stock the men if needed. Convict Furlow had failed to work to satisfy the guard when upon he ordered him in the stocks; he being placed in the stocks by another convict "Hill". This squad of men were at work in the field; when the stocking took place. I refer you to statement made by the darkies who witnessed the stocking. I do not regard this case more unfortunate than others that have happened on other farms but shows clearly how cautious men aught to be when observing (unreadable word) a convict. This is as true an history of the case as I can give and in the future I recommend that no one be permitted to use the stocks but the Sergeant and he to remain in the presence of said convict till sentence is over.

Respectfully submitted, J.T. Gaines, Assistant Inspector
Jan. 26th 1877

[Statement of Witnesses]

I heard Mr. Sumner tell Frank Furlow to get on the stocks which Frank Furlow did. Mr. Sumner told a George Hill to stock the said Furlow which he said George Hill did: he raised the said Furlow until he stood on the balls of his feet he stood in the Stocks about five minutes he then let him down. The said Furlow was not concerned; he then commanded the said George Hill to put him in the stocks again which the said Negro did, after he was put in the second time, he jumped and flayed about to a considerable extent he stayed in the stocks about five minutes and was taken out and found to be dead.

L.E. Whitten and William Lurmen

In the State Inspectors report of March 3, 1877, we find this report of Lake Jackson.

> Lake Jackson Force, February 24, A.O. Shaw, Sergeant
>
> Prison in tolerably good condition. Men get enough to eat but are dirty looking fellows but look very stout and hearty. Clothing needed badly. Shoes only tolerably good. None sick. None complain of bad treatment. Bedding scant and dirty. In ranks 30, Trustees 14, Pardons 1, Discharged 1, Transferred to McNeals 13, Escaped 1, Now in camp 49. Day guards 7, Night do [do=duty guards] 1.

The State evoked this leasing system in 1877 and took back control of the States' prisoners.[7]

During the 1870s, Texas began to increase agricultural production. "By the end of the 1870s the sugar industry in Texas, according to production figures, was recovering from the effects of the Civil War. Although the crop of 1878 was damaged by late rains, the production of the state was 5,664 hogsheads of sugar and 12,224 barrels of molasses."[8] "Brazoria, Fort Bend, Wharton, and Matagorda counties had forty-five sugar plantations in operation by 1880"[9] many relying on convict labor supplied by Cunningham and Ellis.

In 1875, Edward H. Cunningham, a veteran of the Civil War and a wealthy farmer and rancher in Bexar County, while looking for favorable investments, became interested in the sugar plantations in Fort Bend County. He entered into partnership with Col. Littleberry A. Ellis,[10]

---

[7] Walker, 1988: 29-43
[8] Johnson, 1961: 52
[9] Ibid, Page 53
[10] Armstron, R.M. 1991, *Sugar Land, Texas and The Imperial Sugar Company* D. Armstrong Co., Inc. Houston, Texas Page 25

who owned 5300 acres. "It appears that this partnership of Ellis and Cunningham was initially formed partly for the purpose of contracting with the state of Texas for the entire convict population, which they would then sublease to other plantation owners."[11] Their lease contract with the State, included the Huntsville Prison and for each prisoner they were to pay the state $3.01 per month.[12] "In 1880, over half the convicts in the system were being used in Fort Bend and Brazoria Counties. In that year Ellis and Cunningham between them worked 365 convicts, and Cunningham had seven on his Bexar County Ranch."[13] The rest were leased to other plantations.

In the *Biennial Reports of the Directors and Superintendent of the Texas State Penitentiary at Huntsville, Texas with The Report of the Prison Physician, Commencing December 1, 1878 and terminating October 31, 1880,* the following report is found on page 21.

> The question of outside labor, its treatment and attending evils, have been, to some extent, reported upon under the heads of discipline, deaths, and escapes, but there are other points of interest, connected with it, which it may be well to discuss in view of the opposition manifested to it throughout the country.
>
> No one will attempt to deny that the system is an evil, the true reason of which is because of the large mortality attending, the facilities afforded for escapes, and because under it there is little or no chance for reform. It can only be defended on two grounds: necessity, and because it is a source of revenue.
>
> In Texas as in nearly all the other Southern States after the close of the war, on account of the rapid increase of population in prisons and the lack

---

[11] Ibid
[12] Walker, 1988, Page 48
[13] Armstrong, 1991, Page 25

of prison accommodations, the working of convicts outside of the walls became a necessity. In Alabama, Florida and Georgia the entire prison populations is worked outside; in Arkansas, Louisiana and Mississippi a comparative few are kept in the prison, while in Kentucky, South Carolina, Tennessee, Texas and Virginia, a large majority are worked on the outside........

The [Texas] Legislature of 1866 passed a law authorizing employment of convicts on works of public utility. A number were employed under this act in railroad construction, which number was largely increased under the lease of Ward, Dewey & Co.

In 1874 and 1875 most of the convict labor was withdrawn from other outside industries and placed on farms. Up to this time there had been no direct supervision by the State over the convicts at outside labor, in consequence of which there were many abuses, and many instances in which convicts were cruelly and inhumanly treated by those directly over them.

In 1875 Gov. Coke very wisely appointed an assistance inspector to visit outside camps, since which time there has been a constant improvement in the management and treatment of outside convicts under the supervision, first of the assistant inspectors, then of the commissioners, and now of the assistant superintendents. Occasionally now there is an instance of cruel treatment, but these cases are only exceptional. On farms neat, secure and commodious prison-houses, well heated in winter and sufficiently ventilated in summer have been erected, in place of old log pens, the convicts are well clad, well fed, and as a rule, well treated.

In 1882, 1040 prisoners were contracted out in groups to individuals for $15.00 per prisoner per month. The lessee had to furnish housing, food and guards. Lessees were entitled to 10 hours of work per day per prisoner.[14] The *Biennial Reports of the Penitentiary Board and*

---

[14]Walker, 1988, Page 71

of the Texas State Penitentiary : 1882, list the Darrington Plantation with 28 convicts and the Lake Jackson Plantation with 36.[15] In 1883, the State decided to take over the leasing system and take back control of their prisoners. The State had about 3000 prisoners and two prisons, Huntsville and Rusk, that could only hold about 1600 between them. In 1884, 1128 prisoners were leased to private individuals or farms. An additional 176 inmates worked on railroad construction crews.[16]

On Page 7 of the *Reports on the Condition of the Texas State Penitentiary For The Year 1884*, the following information is listed.

> Under the contract entered into between ex-Governor Davis, on the part of the State, and Messrs. Ward, Dewey & Co., the present lessees, the labor and general management of the convicts passes from the State to those gentlemen, subject, however, to the supervisory control of the Board of Directors and myself [Inspector. J.K.P. Campbell].
>
> | | |
> |---|---|
> | In the various industries in and around the prison proper. | 676 |
> | In agriculture and brick making on the Lake Jackson and Patton plantations, in Brazoria County | 314 |
> | In agriculture on the Alston farm, in Walker County | 77 |
> | At the Prison Tannery, In Walker County | 131 |
> | On the various railroads | 255 |
>
> Most of those employed in agricultural pursuits are the Negro convicts, and I have visited all the detachments at a distance from the Penitentiary regularly, and made a thorough inspection of the labor required of the convicts and in no case have I found onerous or excessive tasks imposed, and, but for the prison garb, there is no observable difference between them and free men engaged in the same kind of labor, except that the convict seems better clothed, fed, and in better health.

---

[15] Johnson, 1961, Page 43
[16] Walker, 1988, Pages 90-91

In the official records, the last listing for convicts at Lake Jackson was for November 1, 1884 with a total of 33 convicts.

In 1892, the State leased 1,039 prisoners for $17 per month per prisoners on sugar plantations, $16.50 for prisoners on sugar and cotton plantations, and $15.50 for cotton and corn plantations.[17] In 1886, the State bought the Harlem Plantation in Fort Bend County to be run as a prison farm using convict labor. In 1899 the State acquired 5,527 acres in Brazoria County and acquired the adjoining land of the Lowood plantation with 2,685.47 acres to establish the Clemens Prison.[18] The Lowood plantation was the largest sugar producer in Brazoria County for several years before the Civil War and had some of the finest land in the Brazos River valley. The State continued to acquire land for additional prison farms and in 1912 ended the convict lease system, installing all state prisoners on State owned prison farms.[19] The Retrieve Plantation became the Retrieve prison and the Darrington Plantation, the Darrington prison. This removal from the public market of access to forced labor brought about the decline of sugar production in Texas.[20]

http://web.mac.com/joan_few

---

[17] Walker, 1988, Page 93
[18] Ibid, Page 99
[19] Ibid, Page 100
[20] Ibid

VIII

Excavating Nineteenth Century Sugar Mills

There are no Nineteenth Century sugar mills standing in Texas. The few that are left are in ruins. In 1858, there were approximately thirty-two mills operating in Brazoria County, three mills in Matagorda County, and two in Fort Bend County.[1] Today, two sugar mill ruins are open to the public, the Varner-Hogg State Park and the Lake Jackson State Archeological Landmark Site, owned by the Lake Jackson Historical Association. The Lake Jackson mill is important because it documents the changes in nineteenth century sugar technology and process. Excavations of the Lake Jackson mill began in 1992 with members of the Brazosport Archaeological Society and students from the University of Houston Clear Lake (UHCL). In 1994 and 1995, the Texas Archeological Society held their field schools at Lake Jackson and accomplished most of the fieldwork. Students from UHCL and volunteers completed excavation units at the sugar mill started by the TAS Field Schools.

The best preserved sugar mill ruins in Texas are at the Osceola plantation which is on private land. The owners allowed us to photograph, map and measure the sugar mill ruins and conduct very limited excavations to identify the structural components. This study made it possible for us to identify the components of other sugar mill ruins.

The Osceola plantation was part of the original grant of James Brown Austin the son of Moses Austin and the brother of Stephen F. Austin. His widow was Eliza M. Westall Austin, the daughter of Thomas Westall. Eliza Austin's second husband, Phillips, died at a young age. As a

---

[1] Champomier, P.A. 1852-58 *Statement of the Sugar Crop Made in Louisiana in 1852-58*, Cook, Young and Co. New Orleans

wealthy, twice widowed young lady, she married her third husband, Colonel William G. Hill, in 1836. The Hills established their first plantation, Waverly, and their second plantation, Osceola, on land she inherited from her first husband.[2] Abner J. Strobel in his narratives stated that a Mr. Spofford of New York developed the sugar mill at Osceola,[3] probably after 1865.

The boiler, boiler chimney, engines and cane crushers are the components of the first phase of sugar processing; the extraction of the juice from the sugar cane. The foundations for these components are substantial structures and are in excellent condition at Osceola. The boiler at Osceola is 28 feet in length and in excellent condition. The boiler produced the steam that powered the sugar cane crushers. The boiler chimney is approximately 45 feet tall. The height of the chimney "pulled" the heat through the boiler. Two feet of alluvial fill covers the base of the boiler chimney and the boiler foundation. The chimney is of double wall construction with air spaces between the inner and outer chimney walls. This allowed the inner wall to retain heat to assist with the chimney draft.

Brick foundations supported the cane crushers and the engine that ran the crushers. The better designed sugar mills in Louisiana were two stories high and the size of the Osceola foundations indicates that the engines and crushers were on the second floor. The height allowed the extracted juice to be moved by gravity to the first floor. Almost identical brick supports for engine, flywheel, and cane crushers were found at the Indian Church mill in Belize that operated about 1860 - 1875.[4] The Indian Church mill still has the cane crushers and the engine that

---

[2] McCormick, A. P. 1897, *Scotch-Irish in Ireland and In America, As Shown in Sketches of The Pioneer Scotch-Irish Families McCormick, Stevenson, McKenzie and Bell, In North Carolina, Kentucky, Missouri, and Texas.* Printed by A.P. McCormick, located: Texas State Library
[3] Strobel, 1926, Page 42
[4] Pendergast, D. M. 1982, The 19th-Century Sugar Mill at Indian Church, Belize. IA- *Journal of the Society for Industrial Archaeology,* Vol. 8, No. 1, pp. 57-66

powered the crushers on their original foundations making the identification of these brick structures possible. Lake Jackson had a solid, not arched, brick foundation under the crushers; gears from the crushers at Lake Jackson were found at the base of the crusher foundation during excavations.

Indian Church Sugar Mill in Belize
The Fly Wheel and Cane Crushers Are On Their Original Foundation.
Photo by Donald K. McReynolds

Osceola Boiler and Boiler Chimney

Foundations For the Engine (Left), Fly Wheel and Cane Crushers (Right) at Osceola

The second phase of making sugar is the reduction process; the associated components are the fire, the train of kettles, and the flue chimney. At Osceola these components are 53 feet in length. The heat was produced by a fire under the smallest kettle (about 6 feet in diameter called *la batterie*). The hot air was "drawn" by the height of the flue chimney, through the flue under the kettles exiting up the flue chimney. The lips of the kettles rested on brick supports, which anchored the kettles over the flue. Plenums in the flue kept the heat close to the kettles. The area around and between the kettles was plastered to prevent heat from escaping from the flue. The firebox, flue, kettle supports, plenums and flue chimney are all visible at the Osceola mill.

The firebox at the Osceola plantation had metal "grates" of different sizes and formed a circular shape. The fire was on top of the grates, and the ash dropped below the grates. The smallest kettle was supported by a brick foundation above the fire. The flue, which conducted the heat of the fire under the larger kettles forked at the end of the train and provided heat for two La Grande kettles. Having two kettles made it possible to have one kettle of juice always warmed and skimmed of contaminants ready for the reduction process. The complete process, once started, continued 24 hours a day until the entire sugar crop was processed.[5] If a kettle became too empty and the sugar began to burn, carbonize, then the entire operation had to stop, the kettles cooled and cleaned, and the process restarted. Having a continuous flow of cane juice was critical to the process.

Osceola Firebox With Rubble Filled Flue In the Middle of the Photo

---

[5] Creighton, 1975, Page 200

Flue Entering Flue Chimney at Osceola

The curved bricks in the opening of the flue chimney are an identifying feature. The Lake Jackson sugar mill also has the curved opening of the flue chimney in place.

The final phase of the sugar process was granulation, cooling, and purging, which took place in the purgery. The architectural features of the purgery are: the large space for purging and storage, the interior brick foundations that supported the hogsheads, and a single fire wall or double walls with space between the mill and the purgery for fire protection. The purgery at Osceola was 133 feet long and 47 feet wide. It also contained a plastered vat that was nineteen feet long and eight feet wide; the function of this vat is not known.

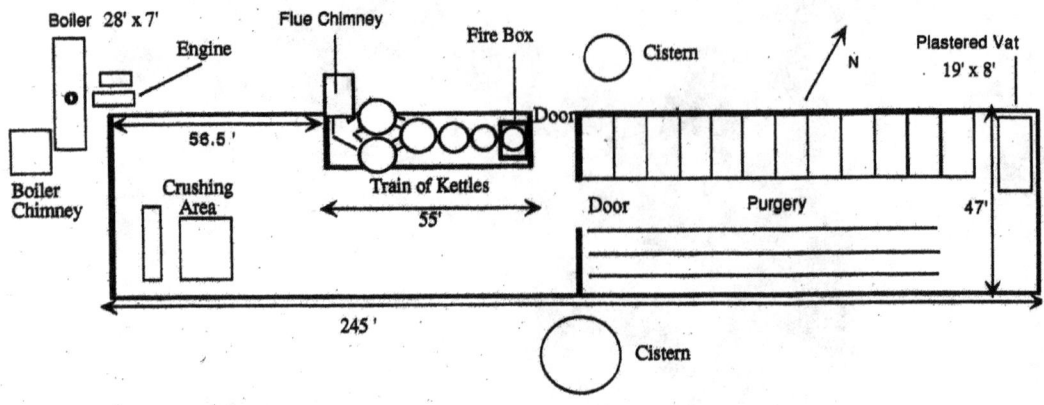

Osceola Sugar Mill

Abner Jackson built his sugar mill in 1848. He selected land, next to Lake Jackson that was slightly elevated above the surrounding area; the natural dike of an old channel of the Brazos River. The location was also close to Oyster Creek to provide transportation for exporting sugar and cotton.

The Lake Jackson Sugar Mill was excavated to answer specific research questions: What was the layout of the original Lake Jackson mill? Was it similar to or different from other sugar mills in Texas? Will excavations support the historic records that document the addition of steam power to operate the cane crushers?

Before the '94 and '95 field schools, the sugar mill was covered with debris and thousands of loose bricks. Members of the BAS, HAS, TAS, students of UHCL, and volunteers spent many weekends carefully removing the brick rubble overburden from the mill.

South Wall of Lake Jackson Sugar Mill During Early Stages of Excavation Note ruler resting on brick in foreground. The circular structure is the lime pit that still contained lime. The mound north of the lime pit is brick overburden from the Dow Chemical road-building process.

The structure on the right is the foundation for the cane crushers that were on the second floor of the mill. On the left are two gears from the cane crushers.

Bands of the Horse Treadmill With Copper Sieve Below Bands

Parts of Horse Treadmill
Bars and Horse Harnesses Resting on the Floor
Next to the Foundation of the Cane Crushers on the Left.

Historical records state that Jackson began the mill using horses to power the cane crushers that extracted the juice from the cane. On the brick floor next to the cane crusher foundation, horse harnesses and large metal bands which supported the treadmill were found.

After the installation of a boiler to produce steam power for the cane crushers, Jackson left the horse treadmill in place to either power the conveyor belt that brought the cane to the crushers or as a back up power source. The foundation of the cane crushers has been identified through comparative studies of other sugar plantations, primarily Osceola. The large metal gears of the cane crushers were also found near the base of their foundation along with fragments of the copper sieve that was placed under the cane crushers to keep plant materials out of the vat that collected the cane juice.

Fragments of Copper Sieve

The foundation for the boilers, engines and pumps installed in 1878 were located just North of the original fire pit. In the early 1900s, The Army Corp of Engineers built a ditch and levee for flood control just south of the plantation site. This operation destroyed all but the north walls of unidentified structures H and J. Other structures may also have been destroyed. In the 1940s, Dow Chemical made the ditch into a fresh water canal "to conduct water from a pumping station on Oyster Creek into a canal system that leads to their local petrochemical complex".[6] During this same period, the Dow Park was built and an access road had to be "squeezed" between the canal and the sugar mill ruins. The southwestern corner of the sugar mill was bulldozed. The

---

[6] Gross, S. et.al. 1989 "Historical Resource Survey of the Lake Jackson Plantation: Survey by the Brazosport Archaeological Society, July 24, 1989

original boiler foundation and boiler chimney may have been in the canal or road area. A possible foundation was discovered in 1994 just east of the foundation for the crusher engine. Next to this feature was discovered a boiler governor. The governor may belong to the Jackson period, or to one of the boilers installed in the Post Civil War alterations.

Kettle Setting: Circular Bricks in Center

Foundation For Cane Crusher, Left. Support For Fly Wheel, Center. Engine Support, Right.

A Photo from the top of the ruins looking east. The kettle settings can be seen, the firebox and the purgery. To the left front is the Jackson flue chimney and the convict boiler foundation.

An inventory of property in 1878[7] documents the change from fire to heat the sugar kettles for the reduction process, to the use of steam as a heat source. It also provides a list of the tools in use at the plantation and has helped identify artifacts.

The inventory lists the following items in use at the sugar mill:

    4 boilers in use at the sugarhouse;
    1 sugar mill [cane crushers];
    1 steam engine;
    4 iron juice boxes;
    5 syrup tanks, iron;
    4 wooden cisterns;
    4 iron coolers;
    1 Gannon steam pump;
    1 Blake steam pump;
    4 iron clarifiers;
    2 copper pans,

---

[7] Brazoria County Deed Q557

The clarifiers and copper pans constituting with their connections and attachments a "steam train;"
1 iron strike car together with all its pipes, connections, and attachments fastening to and used in connecting with each all of the articles mentioned above;
9 sugar kettles
2 Bbls sulfur
2 Bbls sulfate of lime
9 Bbls lime
1 Bbl cement
1 iron cotton press screw
1 ground stone
1 steel cone mill
1 corn shelter
1 1/2 miles of tram road including the rails, ties fastenings of the same
1 car used on said tram road
50,000 bricks, more or less, being all now on said plantation
100 hogsheads more or less now on said plantation
1 corn stalk cutter
1 lay by
1 mowing machine
4 corn planters
2 flukes
6 Champion plows
6 walking cultivators
5 double shovel plows
23 Brinley plows
4 subsoil plows
4 hand saws
1 framing saw
2 cross cut saws
1 lot blacksmith tools
7 cane carts
2 Bagasse carts
1 water cart
3 ox wagons
1 lot wagon wheel
1 oil tank
portions of a sawmill but no saw
23 axes
11 shovels
17 weeding hoes
14 cane hoes
25 picks and mattocks with and without handles

    1 road scraper
    2 bars round iron
    2 bars flat iron
    6 long handled shovels
    24 cane knives
    All mattresses, blankets and articles of bedding used by guards and convicts on plantation. The knives, forks, spoons, cups, plates, and all articles used in cooking for them.
    500 bushes of corn, more or less being all the corn on the place
    1 boot
    3 sows
    15 pigs
    2 yokes of oxen
    1 horse
    28 mules
    plow and wagon gear for plows including whittle trees, harnesses, trace chains, etc.
    1 lot wheelbarrow

TAS excavations discovered that after the Civil War, the mill was substantially altered from Jackson's original construction.

It is important to understand how Jackson period construction and convict labor period construction were identified in the sugar mill.

Several attributes identify Jackson construction:

    Bricks are uniform in size; systematically produced

    Bricks are high in quality; paste is homogeneous, clay is dense, and firing is regular

    Whole bricks are used in construction

    Bricks in foundations and walls are very level

    Quality of the masonry is excellent

During the Convict Labor Period, construction attributes include:

    Bricks are different sizes

    Whole and half bricks are used together in construction

Bricks are poor in quality; paste is not homogeneous, bricks are porous and friable, firing is irregular

Foundations and walls slope and buckle

Masonry is very poor; bricks are not level, mortar is uneven and sometimes excess mortar is not removed to provide a smooth vertical surface (called "bleeding" mortar)

A Perfect Example of Convict Construction
Boiler Foundation For Convict Sugar Mill

Evidence of alterations made by convict labor after 1873 include:

Blocked Passageways: A blocked doorway was found in the wall separating the kettle area from the purgery. The east side of the wall shows an enclosed portal with plastered walls, while the west side has very sloppy, and uneven rows of bricks with "bleeding" mortar. The door between the crusher foundations and the kettle area was also closed with a brick wall.

Raised Walls: The east/west wall, the south wall of the Jackson kettle enclosure, is an excellent example of a raised wall. Attached to the Jackson wall, iron masonry braces were placed about every four or five feet and a new section of wall was added. This alteration may be a result of the change from fire heat (train of kettles) to steam heat (steam train). The upper portion of the train of kettles would have been removed to expose the sides of the kettles. After steam coils were wrapped around the kettles, then the kettle area would have been sealed to enclose the kettles and contain the heat. This would explain convict walls on top of plantation walls in the kettle area.

Raised Floors: The lower Jackson floor is like the Jackson foundation and walls in construction; substantial, level, and with excellent masonry. The lime pit and original Jackson floor found in 1994 became the cornerstone for all other Jackson floor identifications. The upper or raised convict floors are uneven. When the floor is of brick, it is one brick thick and of poor masonry construction. Convict period floors are also of dirt and had between 1 - 1.25 feet of fill between the Jackson floor and the convict floor.

Blocked Chimney: The flue chimney opening was closed by bricks and was separated from the kettle area by a brick wall during the Convict Period alterations.

Firebox removed: The brick foundation and grates of the firebox were removed and the opening to the firebox on the north wall was closed with a brick wall.

In the lower left, is the lime well from the Jackson period and the Jackson floor. To the right is a doorway between the mill proper and the purgery that was sealed during the convict period. The wall in the center shows how the convicts built their wall on top of the Jackson wall using metal bars to stabilize their addition.

Convict Period Boiler Foundation
In the foreground is a pipe draining from the convict period boilers into Lake Jackson. In the center are the metal plates on the brick foundation to support the boilers of the "steam train."

Alteration of Jackson Flue Chimney During Convict Period
The flue chimney was no longer needed and trash was
dumped in the area. Note the metal bar from the Jackson firebox,
exactly like those used in the firebox at Osceola.

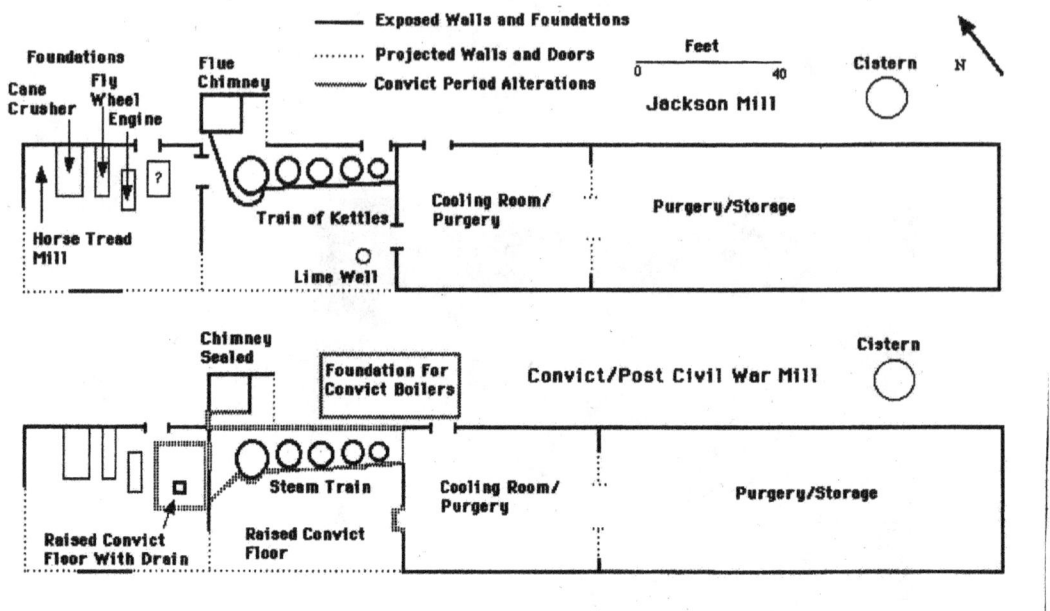

Changes Between the Jackson Mill and the Convict Mill
Train of Kettles (Fire Heat) to Steam Train (Steam Heat)

One of our most important documentations of the history of the mill came from the profile of the north wall of Block 54N/927E, the Block just east of the flue chimney. In this profile, the Indian shell midden can be seen; about one inch above the midden is the 1848 ground surface when the mill was constructed. This area was not a part of the building, but being next to the flue chimney received an ash deposit. Above the Jackson period ash is debris deposited about 1873. The change to the "steam train" made the flue chimney obsolete and the area near the chimney was walled off from the main mill and became a trash area. Above the trash is ash from the Convict Period boilers that were just to the East of this area. Above this ash can be seen bricks with white wash, part of the collapsing of the mill after the 1900 hurricane that devastated the structure. Capping the deposits is a collapsed metal tank.

Excavation Block N54/E927 Profile

Eighty percent of the artifacts found at the sugar mill were bottle glass, nails, window glass and unidentifiable metal. Activity artifacts found in the sugar mill were: the rollers of the cane crusher; gears of the cane crusher; pipes and fittings; the governor of a steam boiler; wire cables; a spade blade; an iron hoe; copper plate; a mason's trowel; a blacksmith's punch; a cane knife; perforated copper sheeting; ball valves; elbow joints; a Texas Department of Corrections hoe; a plow; the top of an oil can or gasket; a shut off valve with an ornate handle; a mica schist "whetstone;" a gas engine fuel filter; metal strip fragments and barrel bands; Haymes harnesses; a copper skimmer; large pieces of metal which were probably parts of vats; and a round brick gaming piece.

Twenty personal artifacts were found, including a plastic folding comb, a slate pencil, a china doll's arm, a snuff can lid, a snuff box, an aspirin box, three nickels (1833, 1926 and 1944), a Walking Liberty Half Dollar, a knife, a key, a compass part, three clay smoking pipe fragments, and an unidentified effigy pipe fragment.

Our excavations did answer our original research questions. By comparing the Lake Jackson mill to three other nineteenth century mills, Osceola, Varner-Hogg and Bynum we can see that these four mills in Brazoria County are very similar in design and layout. We can assume they were similar in process. Our excavations showed the dramatically different building techniques between Jackson and convict construction making it possible to identify the architectural changes that were made to support the technological changes in sugar making.

What was the advantage in changing to steam heat? Henry S. Olcott, an authority on sugar production, wrote in 1857, "Steam does not discolor the sugar nearly so much as fire, therefore steam trains have been extensively adopted, and great expense has frequently been incurred in altering the arrangement of the boiling-house to suit the new *regime*. A steam train will cost twice as much to run and keep in order as a common train will, to say nothing of the first expense..."[8] Olcott also describes the several different ways that steam coils and pipes could be arranged to heat the kettles. Many mill operators claimed the heating of the kettles was easier to control, but workers had to be highly trained to make the process work.

---

[8] Olcott, H.S. 1857, *Sorgho and Imphee, The Chinese and African Sugar Canes*, A.O. Moore, Agricultural Book Publisher, New York, Page 103

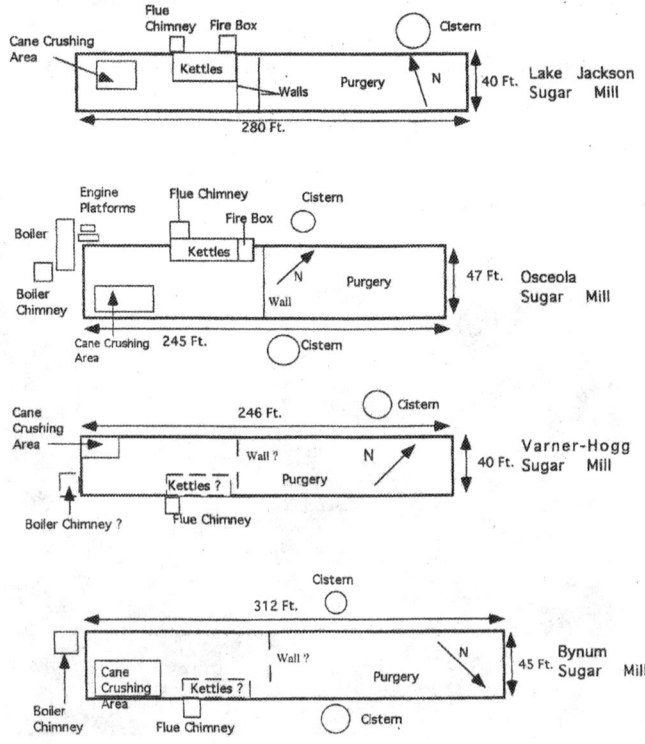

Four Nineteenth Century sugar Mills in Brazoria County

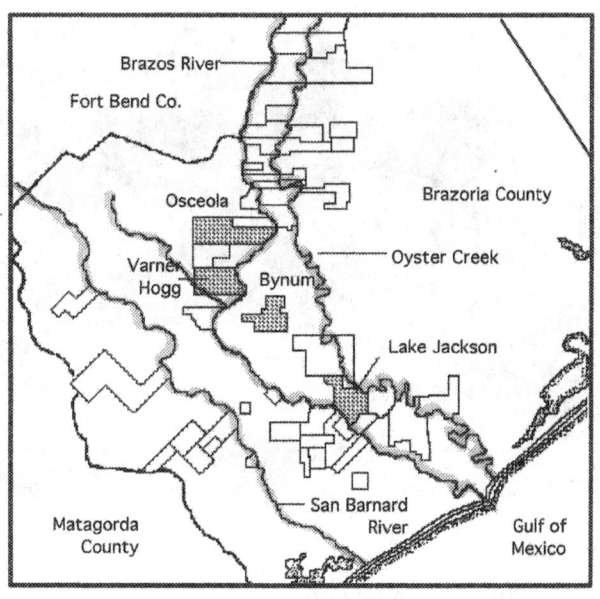

Because so many Texas sugar mills have been completely destroyed or are in ruins, and because the historical record is incomplete, we do not know how many sugar mills changed to the "steam train" method. The Lake Jackson mill may be the only mill in Texas with this technological information available for study archaeologically.

Sugar Mill Excavations

http://web.mac.com/joan_few

IX

Excavation of the Lake Jackson Plantation Main House and Associated Structures

Before excavation could begin a thorough search of all existing documents about nineteenth century Texas sugar plantations was conducted. The historic documents available about plantation history in Brazoria County include public records (censuses, tax records, probate records), plantation journals and records, agricultural journals, diaries and letters, travel journals, newspapers and publications. After researching these documents we formulated questions on what wasn't known about plantation life and what we could learn through archaeology. Our research questions dealt with how structures were constructed; when they were constructed; and what activities took place in and around them.

The archaeological integrity of the main house was unfortunately very low. Local mythology nurtured the idea that gold was buried under or near the main house during the Civil War. The area inside the ruins of the main house is covered with holes dug by people looking for gold. The area is so disturbed that archaeological excavation would not produce reliable information regarding many of our research questions. Excavation around the main house was limited to undisturbed areas.

In the main house area, we laid out a grid of one foot squares to record everything that was found and the exact location. Excavation units in the main house area were 3 by 3 feet. Units were labeled by their southwest corner coordinates.

An artifact pattern is the arrangement and type of artifacts. We are assuming that every social system has identifiable survival strategies; that every survival strategy has a limited amount of energy and resources; that every household and business reflects the whole system through objects used; that all systems are reflected in patterns; and that patterns can be identified in the archeological record by: (1) artifact numbers (how many), (2) artifact association (what with), and (3) artifact distribution (where).

We used Stanley South's[1] method of identifying quantitative patterns by artifact type. South's system applies to all historic sites. The artifact groupings quantitatively identify the specific patterns of cultural function, whether the site is a plantation, farm, factory, fort, urban or rural site.

All artifacts found were grouped according to specific functions: kitchen artifacts include all storage, cooking and eating utensils, and all bottles including pharmaceuticals; bone (food); architecture includes window glass, nails, bolts, all construction hardware, door locks, etc.; furniture includes hinges, knobs, drawer pulls and locks, curtain pulleys, mirrors, chimney lamps, etc.; arms includes bullets, shot, gun flints, gun parts, bullet molds; clothing includes buttons, buckles, thimbles, scissors, pins, beads, etc.; personal includes coins, keys, and personal items (combs, jewelry, watches, pencils, pens, etc.); activities includes construction tools, farm tools, toys, fishing gear, stable and barn objects, miscellaneous hardware (unidentified metal); miscellaneous includes everything that does not fit into any other group and twentieth century

---

[1] South, Stanley, 1977 *Method and Theory in Historical Archaeology,* Academic Press, New York

garbage.[2] Long before the plantation was built, Indians camped in the area; Indian artifacts were grouped together in their own artifact group.

All artifacts were counted and grouped: (1) by level to reflect a level pattern to determine what activities may have taken place in the same place at approximately the same time; (2) by excavation unit to reflect the unit pattern to determine if similar or different activities took place in the same place over time; (3) by structure to reflect a structure pattern to determine how the structure was used; (4) by room to reflect a room pattern to determine how a room was used; (5) and for the entire site to reflect the site pattern of a 19th century cotton-sugar plantation.

Artifact Types at Lake Jackson

Artifact Type	Number	Percent
Kitchen	15,952	20.2%
Bone	12,550	15.9%
Architecture	41,834	53.1%
Furniture	89	0.1%
Arms	183	0.2%
Clothing	724	0.9%
Personal	200	0.3%
Activities	5,664	7.2%
Prehistoric	285	0.4%
Miscellaneous	1,301	1.6%
Total	78,782	

---

[2] Ibid, Page 95

Artifact Types by Structures

Artifacts[3],[4]   Structures: MH (Main House), A, B, C, D, SM (Sugar Mill), I

	MH	A	B	C	D	SM	I
Kitchen	18.5%	25.1%	12.6%	55.5%	24.2%	24.6%	18.9%
Ceramics	110	23	35	10	44	14	5
Bone	7.1%	37.5%	43.7%	7.7%	44.3%	3.7%	12%
Architecture	69.7%	17.4%	32%	26.1%	24.4%	47.3%	22.9%
Furniture	0.1%	0.1%	0.3%	0.2%	<0.1%	0.1%	0.2%
Arms	0.2%	0.3%	0.4%	0.7%	0.3%	0.1%	0.2%
Clothing	0.8%	0.3%	2.3%	0.8%	1.5%	0.3%	0.4%
Personal	0.2%	0.1%	0.5%	0.6%	0.2%	0.2%	0.3%
Activities	3.1%	15%	2.9%	5.7%	1.6%	21.8%	35.3%
Prehistoric	<0.1%	0.7%	0.8%	0.2%	2.4%	<0.1%	0.2%
Miscellaneous	0.3%	3.3%	4.5%	6.3%	5.8%	1.6%	9.9%
Total # of Artifacts	44,935	5,364	8,829	1,333	5,526	8,388	1,159

The main house was identified by its large size. The ruins of the other structures around the main house were much smaller and their uses unknown. We made the assumption, that the highest numbers of arms, furniture, clothing and personal artifacts would be found in the structures where people lived. The arms artifacts found around Structures A, C, D, and I were

---

[3] 99% of all kitchen artifacts were bottle glass fragments; mostly beer bottles.
[4] Ceramics are given by number. Pollan, Sandra D. 1999, *The China Cabinet at the Jackson Plantation: Ceramic Analysis from the Lake Jackson State Archeological Landmark Site (41BO172)* TAS *Bulletin*, Vol. 70, P. 521

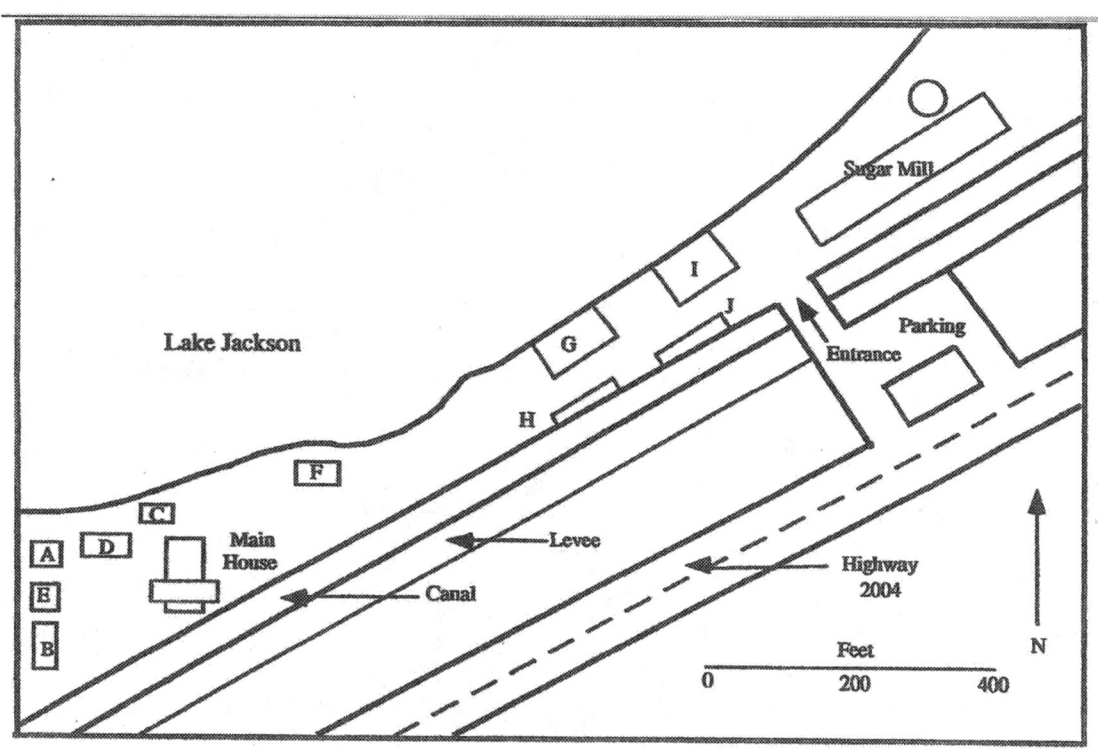

Lake Jackson State Archeological Landmark Site (41BO172)
A-Convict Period, Storage Structure; B- Jackson Period, Altered During convict Period; C- Jackson Period, Wash House; D- Convict Period; E and F - Un-excavated.

close to the surface and date to the Dow Chemical Company Park period. Clothing artifacts, personal artifacts, and ceramics were concentrated at the main house and structures B and D, therefore, we can assume people lived there. Structure B was constructed during the Jackson period, and Structure D, after the Civil War during the convict labor period. Structure A was a storage building constructed after the Civil War and Structure C was a wash house constructed during the Jackson period.

Abner Jackson Strobel in his narratives, described the house, built in 1851, as a twelve room, two-story structure with an exterior of plastered brick. Around the house were orchards and gardens with brick walkways. The west side of the main house was chosen for excavation because this side of the house faced a number of ruins arranged in a manner suggesting that they functioned in association with the main house. One of our objectives was to identify the plantation period ground living surface. To do this, we looked for evidence of walkways, garden borders, and brick roadways.

Excavations in research area A, at the west side of the front porch of the main house, focused on uncovering the step area and locating the drive and walkways around the main house. The front walkway/driveway was discovered with bricks of excellent quality, laid in a curved pattern. The house faced south toward the Brazos River.

Other features in the area of the front porch also document the ground surface level of the Jackson period. Just west of the front steps, a brick border was located. Just to the east of the brick border, between the front steps and the border, was a layer of Rangia shells all turned bulb, or outside, up. This same configuration of shells was found off the back porch below the convict period walkway and next to the Jackson period walkway.

On the back side of the main house (the north side), the foundation was exposed down to its base. The level where the foundation joined the structure was the same level as the plaster base on the front porch that established ground level during the plantation period.

Off of the west back porch, a convict period sidewalk was found above a Jackson period walkway. This uneven convict walkway of poorly made whole and half bricks, one brick layer in depth, raised the walking area about six inches above the Jackson walkway and extended out from the back porch toward the cistern and Structure D.

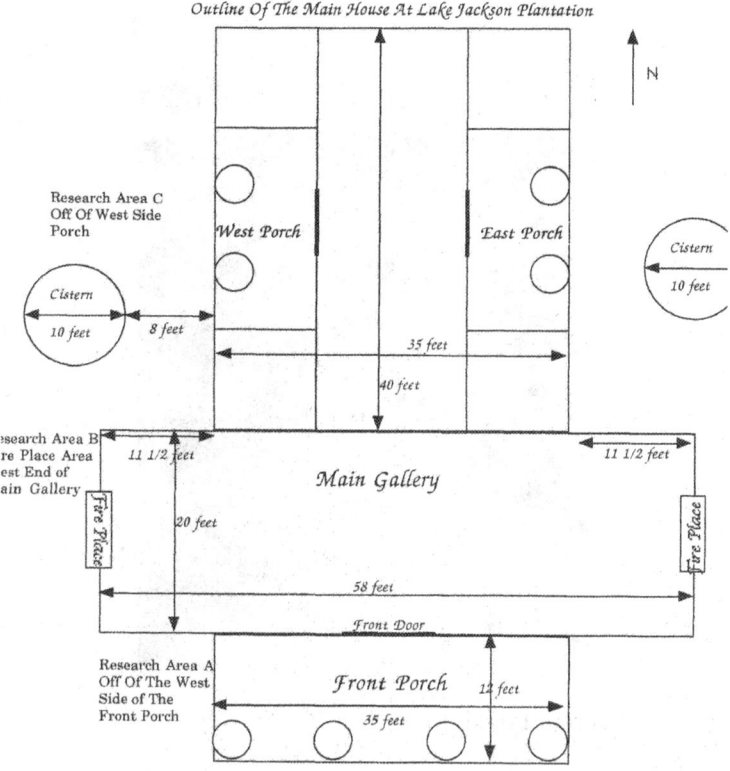

1890s Photo of the Plantation Main House Courtesy of the Brazoria County Historical Commission

Front Porch, Plantation House, West Side

The remnants of a circular pillar can be seen on the left corner of the porch. The curved bricks and plaster can be seen as well as the curving bricks of the front walkway.

Triangular Bricks In Porch Columns

Artifacts between 1.5-2.0 feet below surface appear to be a mixture of the Jackson period and the late 19th century occupation. Deposits from 2.0-3.0 feet below surface are in the Jackson period. The artifacts, especially ceramics, buttons, and datable objects in the lower levels of excavation were manufactured in the 19th century. Ceramics located in research area A, in level five, ranged in age from 1847-1896, and in level six from 1838-1879[5]. The type of clay in the area would make for easy "percolation" of small artifacts moving up and down within the soil thus making a clear line of distinction difficult between occupations. Most artifacts excavated at the Main House were found between one to two feet below the surface.

The front steps of the main house are an example of the quality of masonry and construction in the Jackson period. The specially designed bricks used in construction are *in situ*.[6] The edge of the front porch and the edge of the three steps ascending the front porch are rounded. The rounded edge is also found in the two steps of the west side back porch. The front porch step area is of solid whole bricks, some laid on their sides for additional strength. A curved brick pattern can be seen in the front walkway/driveway. Plaster covered the steps and was still in place under the curved edge bricks.

Another architectural feature of the porches are the columns. There are four columns across the front porch and two columns on the back west porch. These columns included triangular bricks. In the columns, triangular bricks alternated with hand-shaped bricks, bricks made whole but shaped by the mason to fit a specific place. This configuration of triangular and shaped bricks formed the circular shape.

---

[5] Ibid

[6] "in situ" - a phrase meaning that the objects are in the exact place/location where they were used.

The area around the fireplace located in the main front room (Main Gallery) of the west side of the house was excavated. The hearth indicated the level of the floor in the house.

The floor of the house is assumed to be of wood with the floor approximately three feet above the ground. A crawl or "ventilation" space was located between the floor and the ground as evidenced by the metal vents found on each side of the fireplace and in each of the north and south walls by the fireplace. The hooks for the grates that covered the vents are still in place on both sides of the west fireplace.

The back porch on the west side of the main house is a smaller version of the front porch, having two columns instead of four and two steps instead of three. The columns are identical in size to those on the front porch and the steps are identical with the decorative curved bricks on the edge of the steps. Columns and steps were plastered on both porches.

Personal artifacts found off the back porch provide a glimpse of the possessions of the people living and visiting the main house during the Convict Labor Period dating from 1873 to 1900. The Robert Glass family were the last people to live in the main house. Mr. Glass had been "hired by the state to fix up buildings at the Lake Jackson Plantation." The Glass family was living in the house during the 1900 hurricane, when they lost most of their possessions according to an oral history by Mrs. Rae Glass Smith (born 1891).[7]   Mrs. Smith recalled that the ground was covered with mud after the storm. Some of the personal artifacts found in this back porch area that may have belonged to the Smith family include a ring, a 1893 penny, slate pencils, a key, a metal purse clasp, the lid to a cream jar, a pin (jewelry), a stone pipe fragment, the back of a pocket watch with the serial number 2330835, a rubber comb with an 1851 patent

---

[7] Personal correspondence with Jamie Murray, 6-19-94 (Oral history interview by Jamie Murray in 1976) Oral History Tape in Collections at the Brazoria County Historical Museum.

date, harmonica parts, pieces of a china doll head (found in five different excavation units) and a piece of shell jewelry. Also found was a 1945 nickel.

More bones were recovered in the excavations around the main house than from any other structure. Bones of cows and pigs are equally represented, along with chicken. Deer, turkey, fish, turtles, birds, rabbits and squirrels are also prominent.[8]

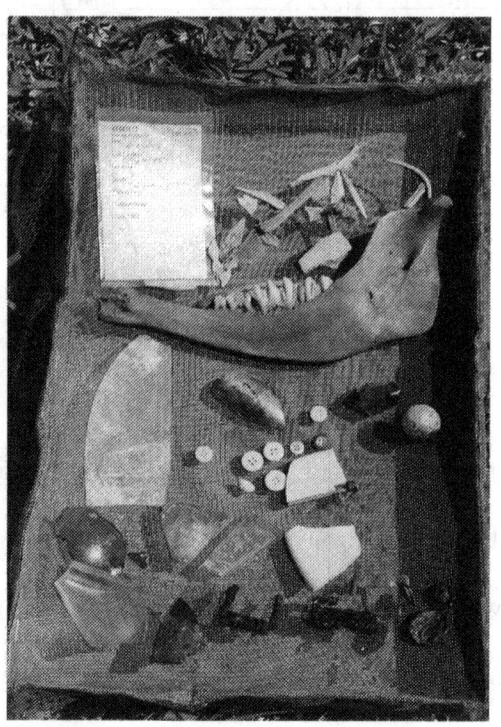

Artifacts From a Unit in Research Area A of the Main House

Unit S90/W25, Level 3, Bag Number: 1073
These artifacts have been washed and are in the process of drying on wire mesh, stretched over a card board box.
Bone fragments are seen at the top, buttons and two large ceramic pieces in the center. The small ball is a bottle stopper. A large window glass fragment is on the left. At the bottom are bottle fragments and metal pieces.

---

[8] McClure, W. L. "The Vertebrates from lake Jackson State Archeological Landmark" *Bulletin of the Texas Archeological Society* Vol. 70, 1999, Page 531

Structure A

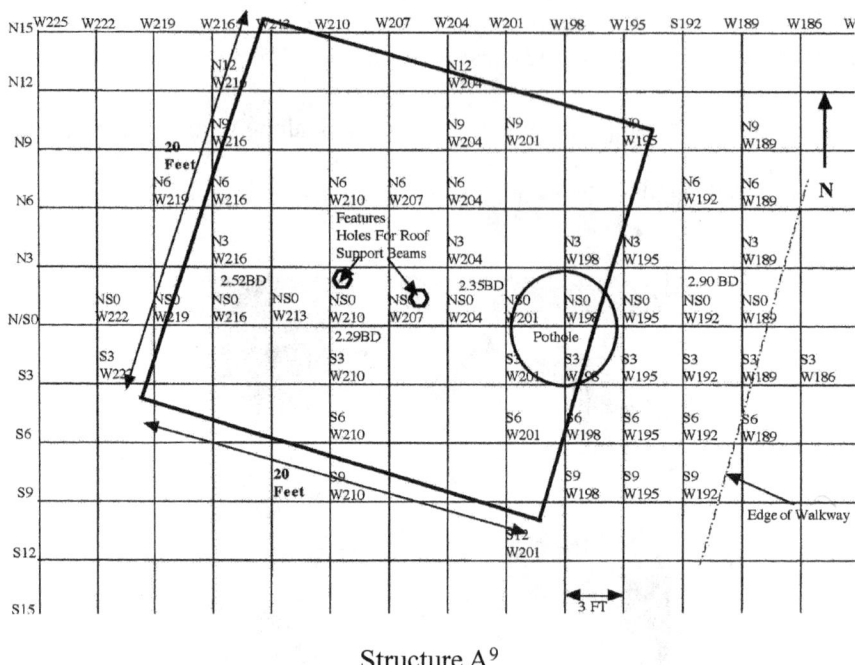

Structure A[9]

Structure A was the first structure at Lake Jackson to be excavated. During the construction of the Dow Chemical Company park, the standing ruins of this structure were cleared and grass was allowed to grow over the leveled structure. As grass was cleared from the area, a 20 X 20 foot structure with its brick floor intact was found. Outside the structure, on the east side, a brick walkway was discovered that had been constructed like the convict walkway on the East side of the main house.

The only artifacts in situ, were found east of the structure between the fallen east wall and the Convict Period (about 1873) walkway. These artifacts were mostly activity artifacts which included a wagon wheel hub, fragments of a metal plow, a horse shoe, a metal ring, hooks, a pipe

---

[9] On the eastern side, a circle shows the location of a "pothole." A hole dug by someone looking for buried treasure or prehistoric vessels.

wrench jaw, a cast iron frame for a pulley, a hatchet head, a T shaped rail, a stove bolt with nut, a large metal chain, a cutter blade, gear fragments with 10 teeth, and a metal cylinder. A Yale lock was found that had a date of 1878. Cup fragments of a white granite ware were found in this area with a Holland mark that circulated between 1850-1890.[10]

There are several structural aspects that lead to the conclusion that Structure A, is a post Civil War structure: the bricks are not uniform and are a different size from the main house bricks; main house bricks are whole bricks but in Structure A, whole and half bricks were used; the masonry at the main house is solid and the mortar cleaned but in Structure A, the mortar was allowed to "bleed," and was not cleaned off of the sides of the foundation; the interior foundation does not have "steps" which are found in plantation period buildings; and the exterior walkway on the east side of Structure A matches the Convict Period walkway at the main house in brick type, quality, and size.

Artifacts found in Structure A date from the post Civil War era to 1900. This supports the conclusions drawn from its structural aspects. The artifacts also support the idea that this may have been a storage structure. All of the artifacts in situ are activity artifacts that would have been kept in a barn or storage structure.

Structure B

Structure B is a three room brick structure with the exterior covered with whitewashed plaster; the interior with whitewash on brick. The three rooms are A (north room), B (middle room with brick floor), and C (south room). The exterior measurements of the structure are 30

---

[10] Pollan, 1999

feet by 15 feet. Rooms A and B were partially destroyed during the construction of a drainage ditch dug during the construction of Dow Park (1945). Structure B was built during the Jackson

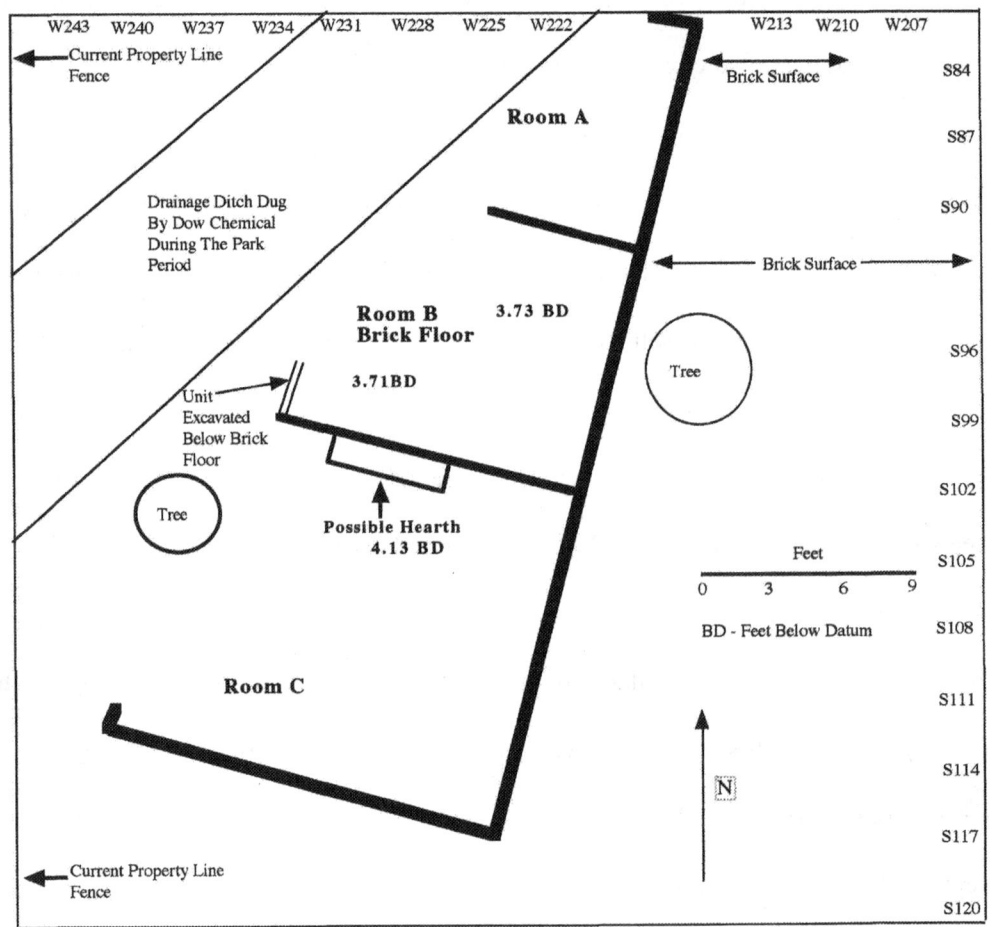

Structure B

plantation period. A brick exterior surface/walkway was found east of the structure. These walkway bricks appear to be from the Convict Period (1873 - 1900).

The total number of artifacts uncovered in Structure B was 8829. Artifacts found in Room A totaled 356; in Room B, 513; and in Room C, 6,567. More of Room C was excavated than

Rooms A and B. Room B had a brick floor that we chose not to remove, and Room A had been badly damaged in the construction of the drainage ditch.

In Room C artifact counts were highest in levels 5 and 6; in the main house they were highest in levels 3 and 4. The clothing artifacts include a Louisiana militia button of vest size with a pelican on the front, and "extra quality" on the back. This button was manufactured just before the Civil War in 1859 and 1860.[11] A thin gold coating on the button is still visible. The other 173 buttons found in Structure B were of china and bone that would have been used on cheap clothing, the type worn by slaves and house servants.[12] There were other types of clothing artifacts found in Room C that suggest a domestic living area: a brass shoe tap, scissors, hooks and eyes, buckles, a brass shoe eyelet, beads, a metal thimble, and a copper thimble.

The personal artifacts in the room also suggest that this was a domestic living space: a watch crystal, chain, two coins, slate board fragment, a slate pencil, seven fragments of clay pipes, a rubber comb (May 6, 1851 patent date), a 1860 Seated Liberty Dime, part of a pocket knife, a pocket knife blade, several pieces of broken jewelry, a copper harmonica reed, and a brass medal pendant. The round pendant has an eye on the top, a male figure on one side that could be either Mercury or Perseus, wearing a winged helmet and carrying a raised sword in the right hand and a lowered shield in the left hand. He is striding across water where an immersed sea creature is holding a trident. Written around the edge is "QUIS UT" to the left of the figure and "DUES" to the right of the figure. On the reverse side is a female madonna-looking figure

---

[11] Albert, A.H. 1976 *Record of American Uniform and Historical Buttons: Bicentennial Edition*, Boyertown Publishing Company, Boyertown, PA

[12] Pool, J. 1996 (Chapter 15) "If Buttons Could Talk", (Few 1996) *Final Report of Research and Excavation at the Lake Jackson State Archeological Landmark, Lake Jackson, Texas 41-BO-172, Between 1991 and 1996, Page 157*

with hands crossed at the chest, standing on what looks like a curved pedestal. Around her head are dots representing a halo. Around the medallion is written "TOTA PULCHRA" on the left side and "ANTE SOEGU LAERAM" on the right. In activity artifacts, the presence of children is indicated by a china doll head, marbles, a toy tea pot, and slate pencils. Most activity artifacts are metal objects: some tools and unidentified metal fragments. A large pulley and a nine foot long gear bar in three foot sections were found 1.5 inches above the brick floor in Room B. A roller castor was found beside the bar. The gear bars had fragments of wood and whitewash attached to the back side, showing that it was mounted to wood, possibly on the ceiling.

A bone deposit was in the northeast corner of Room C in an ash deposit. This deposit had several large bovine bones (tibia and scapula) with butcher marks and "edible and non edible parts of bones of domestic stock as well as fish, turtles, rodents, and wild game".[13] The practice of throwing ash and trash to the right of the fireplace and into the corner of the room is similar to the trash deposit found to the right of the hearth in Room A of Structure D. More research into trash deposition in the nineteenth century is needed to explain this behavior.

Along the north wall of Room C, in the center, is a feature, three bricks thick that may represent a hearth. To the right is a one-brick overlay of bricks that abuts a brick ledge along the north wall at the level of the hearth. One possible explanation based also in part on the depth of artifacts in Room B, may be that Room C originally had a dirt or wood floor and was occupied during the Jackson period.

---

[13] McClure, 1999, Page 531

Artifacts By Type - Structure B

Excavated From Rooms A, B, C

Artifact Type	Room A		Room B		Room C	
	#	%	#	%	#	%
Kitchen	41	11.5%	42	8.2%	566	8.6%
Bone	136	38.2%	90	17.5%	3354	51.1%
Architecture	134	37.6%	333	64.9%	1902	28.9%
Furniture	4	1.1%	0	0	17	.26%
Arms	1	.28%	1	.19%	31	.47%
Clothing	1	.28%	3	.58%	185	2.8%
Personal	2	.57%	1	.219%	35	.53%
Activity	16	4.5%	9	1.75%	192	2.9%
Prehistoric	10	2.8%	2	.38%	53	.80%
Miscellaneous	11	3.1%	32	6.2%	288	3.47%
Total	356		513		6567	

Room C was a domestic residence where plantation activities may have occurred. In an oral history given by Mrs. Ray Glass Smith[14], she referred to Structure B as the "jail." This structure could have been enclosed, all but one door sealed, the interior walls removed, and the floors bricked, leaving a large space for confinement.

---

[14] Murray, 1976

Excavated Room C of Structure B
Looking North

On the right, note the interior steps in the foundation typical of Jackson construction.
Along the north wall of the room can be seen the bricks of the hearth.
Note the overlay of the bricks above the hearth, a possible floor from the convict period.
Room B with its brick floor is seen directly north of Room C.
Johnney Pollan and Gary Vickers, Brazosport Archaeological Society,
excavating below the brick floor of Room B.

Structure C

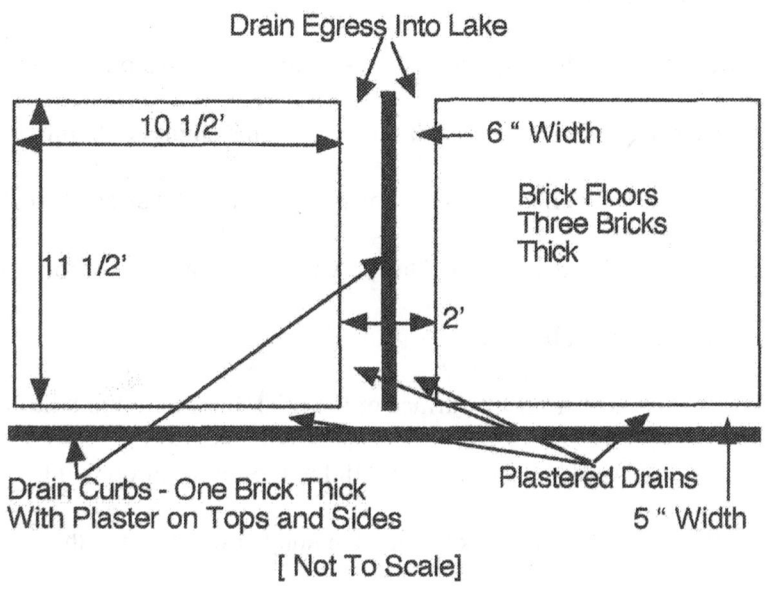

Structure C is located to the north of the main house and on the southern shore of Lake Jackson. Structure C was built during the Jackson period. This is apparent because the structure was built with whole bricks of the same size, the masonry is of fine quality, and the interior foundation of the structure is stepped and of the same type of construction as seen in Structure B and the main house.

Structure C was probably the wash house. It is composed of two brick floor surfaces (10.5 X 11.5 feet) that are surrounded by plastered drains. The drains empty north into the lake. The plaster is the same as that found on the exterior walls of the Main House and Structure B. The drain curbs are also plastered on the sides and tops. Along the south wall of the wash house, abutting the drain curb, is a brick border.

Most of the artifacts came from the surface of the brick floor or around the edges of the structure. Excavations uncovered the structure but did not excavate through it to preserve what was left. A plantation the size of Lake Jackson and the number of people in the Jackson family would require a considerable amount of time for washing linens, clothing, and dishes. Any objects that would fall on this floor during washing activities would have been either picked up, or washed from the floor into the drain and then the lake.

Structure D

Structure D was uncovered in the early spring of 1993 when the road laid by Dow Chemical Company for their company park was removed. The building of the road greatly impacted the structure itself. The road bed was bulldozed to grade, leaving only the foundation of the structure in place. Doorways were not identified. The structure must have had wood or dirt flooring. Artifacts below the road surface were undisturbed and provided information on how the rooms may have been used.

Structure D is a 40 X 20 foot structure with two rooms and two internal fireplaces in the center of the structure. The foundations of the fireplaces are not the same size; the hearth in

Room B is larger than Room A.

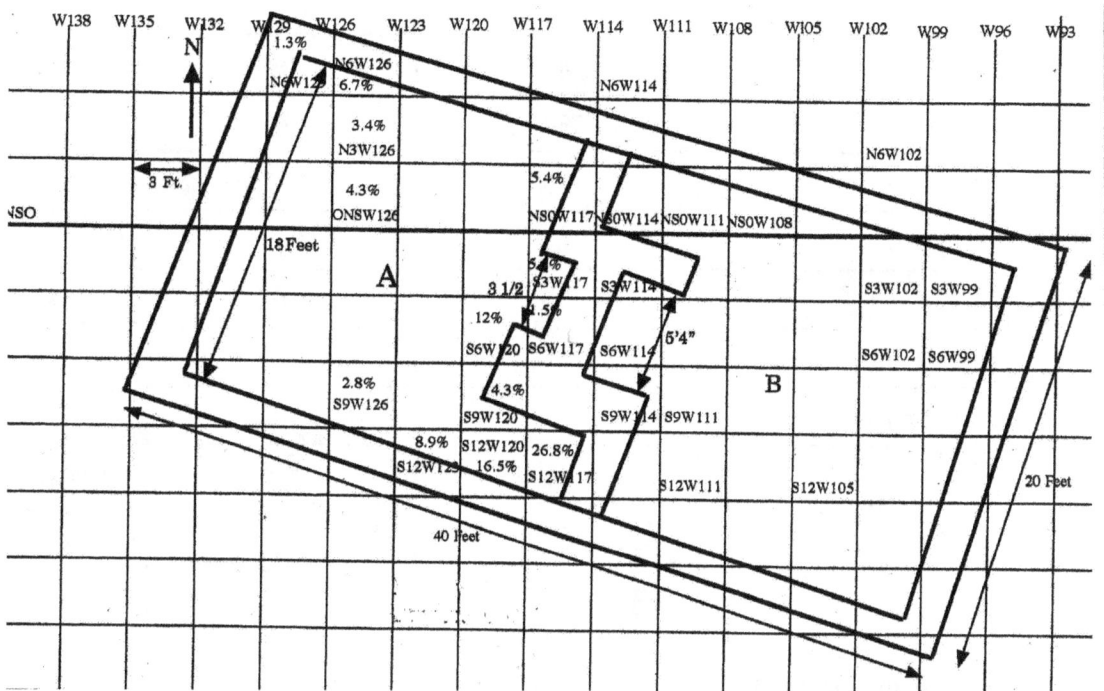

Structure D Showing Rooms A and B and Units Excavated
Unit S12/W117 held 26.8% of the artifacts found in Room A

All artifacts found in the area of Structure D, including all un-provenanced (artifacts found in disturbed areas such as in road construction areas) and surface collections, totaled 5526. Provenanced artifacts, undisturbed by the road building and removal processes, reflect the 19th century occupation and totaled 4725.

Structure D, Provenanced Artifacts

Type	Total	Percentage
Kitchen	902	19%
Bone	2341	49.5%
Architecture	1309	27.7%
Furniture	2	.004%
Arms	16	.03%
Clothing	85	1.79%
Personal	9	.02%
Activities	61	1.2%
Total	4725	

The two rooms, labeled A and B, had different quantities and types of artifacts. In Rooms A and B 13 (3 X 3 foot) units were excavated to sterile levels. Units in both rooms were selected to expose the fireplace hearth area or to randomly investigate the rest of the room. In both rooms some units contained structural components and therefore were not completely excavated.

Provenanced Historic Artifacts in Rooms A and B

Type	A	B
Kitchen	15.2%	30.9%
Bone	55%	39.9%
Architecture	25.6 %	27.8%
Arms	0.3%	0

Clothing	2.2%	0
Personal	0.15%	0
Activities	1.3%	1.3%
Total	3986	446

The kitchen artifacts in Room A include ceramics, a bone handled knife, and two copper forks with silver plate. Architecture artifacts included window glass and round and square nails. Arms included lead shot, a fragment of a ram rod, and a shotgun shell base. Clothing included two buckles and buttons that are primarily china and bone from everyday garments.[15] Personal artifacts included a Seated Liberty U.S. Dime, and clay pipe fragments. Activities included marbles, a porcelain doll face, and a lock with the date of 1878.

The distribution of artifacts in the Room A units indicates a high concentration of debris south of the fireplace. The alcove/closet/cabinet south of the fire hearth contained 26.8% of the artifacts found in Room A and may have served as a trash dump. The largest fragments of ceramics, bone, knives, and forks were found in this deposit. The domestic artifacts suggest that a family lived in Room A during the second part of the 19th century.

Because the same number of units were excavated in Rooms A and B, and in the same general areas, theoretically, differences in artifacts may indicate differences in activities between the two rooms. Differences in the types and quantities of artifacts between the two rooms indicates that the rooms were not used in the same way. Room B may have had a domestic use but it does not reflect the same level of use as Room A. Architectural artifacts were broken

---

[15] Pool, J. 1996

window glass and square and round nails. The activity artifacts in Room B were all unidentified metal.

The bones found in Structure D, included edible and non edible portions of domestic and game animals. "The ratio of bones of fish, birds, rabbits, pigs, deer, and cows at Structure D is comparable to the array of bones from the overseer's house at Eagle Island Plantation. Eagle Island Plantation was the neighbor plantation south of the Lake Jackson Plantation."[16]

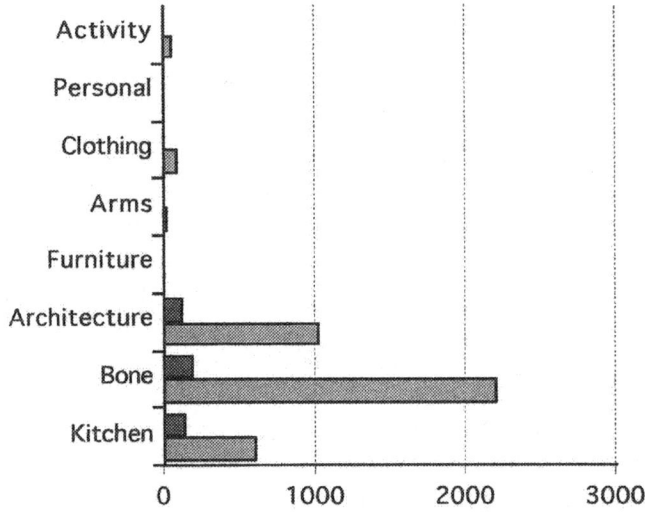

Comparison of Rooms A and B of Structure D
A = Grey and B = Black

Poor construction techniques along with artifacts found in Structure D suggest that this structure was built after the Civil War. Room A may have been occupied by a family, and could also have served as a kitchen for the occupants of the main house. Room B may have served several different functions: office, jail, infirmary, residence or guest quarters.

---

[16] McClure, 1999, Page 531

X.

Archaeological Summary

The Lake Jackson State Archeological Landmark, LJSAL, contains 2.719 acres of the 4642 acre plantation developed by Abner and Margaret Jackson in the late 1840s. The main structures of the plantation were constructed on the south side of Lake Jackson with the residential and industrial areas about 300 feet apart. Historic records document Jackson as one of the largest sugar producers in the state prior to the Civil War. Less than 2 % of the LJSAL has been excavated or tested. Seven structures were partially excavated and 5 additional structures located.

Archeological excavations revealed the original plan of the sugar mill and the discovery of key artifacts and features have defined how sugar was made when the mill was first constructed. Horse harnesses and metal bands found next to the foundation of the cane crushers in the sugar mill give evidence of a horse/mule treadmill as the original source of power for the cane crushers. After steam power was installed to operate the cane crushers, the horse tread mill could have been used to operate the cane conveyor belt which brought the cane to the second story crushers.

Comparative studies of sugar mills in the Brazos River valley support the identification of the foundation of the cane crushers at Lake Jackson. Finding the rollers and gears of the cane crushers on the floor next to the cane crusher foundation verified the identification.

The location of the train of kettles and the flue chimney are evidence that in the early years sugar was processed by heat reduction, fire being the source of heat. Historical records state that after the Civil War, the source of heat used in the reduction process changed from fire to steam, the "steam train" method. This is supported in the archeological record by the extensive architectural alterations made to the sugar mill around 1873: the flue chimney, a critical component in the use of fire for heat, was sealed and walled off from the kettle area; the brick foundations which held the kettles were partially destroyed so that steam coils could be attached to the kettles, the foundations were then rebuilt, resulting in convict-built walls on top of Jackson era slave walls in the kettle area; foundations for the boilers were built north of the original mill to provide steam heat to the kettles; floors were raised; and product traffic patterns, documented by sealed doorways, were altered to accommodate the new reduction process.

The importance of the Lake Jackson site is that it documents the original method with which sugar mills were constructed and contains the structural changes that were necessary to change to the "steam train" method of making granulated sugar. This may be the only mill in Texas where these processes can be studied archaeologically.

The evidence provided by artifacts cannot address the issues of the self sufficiency of the pre Civil War plantation operation because the only provenanced domestic artifacts firmly associated with the Jackson period are the ones in Room C of Structure B. The structure size, location, and the simplicity of the artifacts (cheap buttons and common china) suggests that Structure B may have served as the plantation kitchen and been occupied by slaves/house servants. All of the items found were industrial, not home made. The bricks used in the Jackson buildings were made on site according to historic records. They were of excellent quality. They did not have makers marks but, in some bricks hand prints of the workers can be seen. All of the artifacts found in the sugar mill relating to the sugar making process were imported and industrially made.

The site and its structures were damaged by the 1900 hurricane and by the development of the Dow Chemical Company park, which leveled many of the ruins and built roads on top of others. Even so, the architectural remains of the structures have given the most important cultural information at the site. Foundation construction, size and type of bricks, and quality of masonry have made possible the identification of Jackson period structures, post Civil War structures (Convict period), structural alterations and structure function.

The main house, sugar mill, and Structures B, C and I, were built during the Jackson period. Structures A and D were built during the Convict period. Structures E, F, G, H, and J have not been excavated. The sugar mill was extensively altered after the Civil War. Structure B was altered by sealing doors, adding brick floors and possibly removing interior walls.

Excavations around the main house found convict walkways above Jackson-period walkways. Jackson walkways helped determine the exterior living surface during the Jackson period. The absence or presence of exterior plaster covering the bricks of the main house and the dividing line between foundations and walls also helped determine the exterior living surface. Profiles of builders trenches in the sugar mill, built in the late 1840s, identified the land surface on which the sugar mill was built; these surfaces are the same level as the main house built in 1851.

Buttons, china wares, and bones, when found in situ, can reveal information on activities, status, time, cost, and trade. At Lake Jackson, some of these artifacts types were found in areas that can be associated with the residents of the main house and the residents of Structure D during the Convict period (1873-1900), and the people living in Room C of Structure B during the Jackson period (1851 - 1873). Only one artifact, a Texas Department of Corrections hoe found in the sugar mill, can be associated with the convicts during the Convict Period at the site.

The buttons found date from the 19th century.[1] Buttons were found in all areas of the site but the highest concentrations were at the main house and Structures B and D. Most of the buttons reflect everyday clothes. Buttons from the Victorian period were found at the main house in levels associated with the Convict period of 1873-1900.

The majority of bones[2] were found in areas where surface disturbance, such as site leveling for the construction of Dow Park and the construction of the Dow road, made cultural association difficult if not impossible. Structure B (Jackson period) and the lower levels of excavation in room C, contained domestic (cow, pig and chicken) bones mixed with indigenous wild species of mammal, fish and fowl. The trash deposit to the right of the fire hearth in room A of Structure D (Convict Period) contained a wide variety of domestic and wild animal bones. These two areas in Structures B and D where deposits were undisturbed give us the best view of food resources during the Jackson and Convict periods.

Ceramics found at the site[3] are simple, not expensive wares. Their presence documents British trade wares in Texas during the 19th Century. The wares found in Structures B and D and around the main house give us the best inference to the class and economic status of the residents of Lake Jackson during the Jackson period and later during the Convict Period.

In looking for residential structures, looking at particular artifact types can be helpful. We can hypothesize that furniture artifacts would be found in domestic dwellings as well as arms. Guns and ammunition would not have been unattended but would have been kept in domestic

---

[1] Few, et.al. 1996, *Final Report of Research and Excavation at the Lake Jackson State Archeological Landmark, Lake Jackson, Texas 41BO172, Between 1991 and 1996, Under Antiquities Permit, 1072,* University of Houston Clear Lake, Houston, Texas, Page 158
[2] McClure, W. L. 1999, The Vertebrates from Lake Jackson State Archeological Landmark, *The Bulletin of the Texas Archeological Society,* Vol. 70, Page 525
[3] Pollan, Sandra D. 1999, The China Cabinet at the Jackson Plantation: Ceramic Analysis from the Lake Jackson State Archeological Landmark Site (41BO172), *The Bulletin of the Texas Archeological Society,* Vol. 70, Page 511

areas for defense and protection of the weapon. By comparing where arms and furniture were found, the highest numbers were found in the structures where we believe people lived; the Main House and Structure B. Another way of searching for domestic structures is to look for the highest numbers of clothing artifacts, personal artifacts and ceramics. The highest numbers were found at the Main House, Structure B and Structure D.

The major components of the sugar mill have been exposed and identified. The structural alterations in the mill document the changes in sugar making in the 19th century. The personal and activity artifacts found give a glimpse into the daily lives of the occupants: toys of the children; round gaming pieces of brick found in the sugar mill; a pocket watch, harmonica, simple jewelry, and buttons. All of these artifacts help with a personal visualization of the lives of the occupants. The artifacts from the Dow Park period suggest that picnicking, fishing, beer drinking, and target practice were frequent activities.

Archeological excavations between 1991 and 1998 have added to our knowledge of the sugar industry which dominated the economics of Brazoria County during the 19th century, and the way public park areas were used during the 20th century.

http://web.mac.com/joan_few

XI.

Appendices

Chapter 2:

Sugar Production in Texas, 1852
P.A. Champomier

Brazoria County	Hogsheads
Mills, Robert & David G.	1338
Low Wood Place	780
Bynum Place	558
Jackson, Abner	746
Lake Place	296
Retrieve (Jackson & James Hamilton)	450
Smith, Morgan L. (Waldeck)	520
Sharp, W. (Chenango)	500
McNeel, John G. (Ellerslie)	408
Mims, Sara (Mims)	368
Westall, A.E.	285
Runnels, Hal. G.	270
Perry, James F. (Peach Point)	260
Wharton, Mrs. Sarah A. (Eagle Island)	240
McNeel, Sterling (Darrington)	235
McNeel, P.S.	210
McNeel, Estate of Leader Harrison (Pleasant Grove)	208
Caldwell, James P. (Oakland)	200
Sayre, Charles D.	200
Manor, William	200
Patton, C.R. (Patton/ Varner - Hogg)	210
Bates, Gen. Joseph	160
Black, E.H.	159
Tinsley, Issac J.	140
Bell, T.C. & J.H.	120
Townes, Judge R. J.(Peach Lake)	120
McNeel, Pleasant Duke (Pleasant Grove)	80
Calvit, Mrs. B.M.	70
Sweeny, John	60
Yeiser, D.F.	60
Blanton, Dr.	12

Matagorda County
J.B. & J.D. Hawkins	440
Mills, Power & Warren (Caney Place)	420
Maj. Abram Sheppard	360
Col. P. Hardeman	258
Col. Henry Jones	240
Capt. John Rugely	236
Henry Gibson	160
Estate of G. R. Kemser	125
Mrs. Ann Thompson	60

Wharton County
Gov. A.C. Horton	320
Capt. W.J.E. Heard	140
Eli Mercer	110
James C. Meyers	80

Fort Bend County
Jonathan D. Waters	416
M.F. Williams	168
W.W. McMahan	12

Sugar Production in Texas, 1853
P.A. Champomier

Brazoria County	Hogsheads
Jackson, Abner	727
Lake Place	142
Retrieve (Jackson & James Hamilton)	585
Mills, Robert & David G.	600
Low Wood Place	467
Bynum Place	133
Smith, Morgan L. (Waldeck)	460
McNeel, Sterling (Darrington)	430
Sharp, W.(Chenango)	350
Perry, James F. (Peach Point)	320
McNeel, John G. (Ellerslie)	250
Manor, William	210
Mims, Sara (Mims)	200
Runnels, Hal. G.	200
Westall, A.E.	140
Wharton, Mrs. Sarah A. (Eagle Island)	135
Patton, C.R. (Patton/ Varner - Hogg)	130
Caldwell, James P. (Oakland)	120
Townes, Judge R. J. (Peach Lake)	116

McNeel, Estate of Leader Harrison (Pleasant Grove)	105
Black, E.H.	100
Sayre, Charles D.	100
McNeel, P.S.	95
Hall, W. D. C.	92
Bates, Gen. Joseph	60
Tinsley, Issac J.	60
Yeiser, D.F.	60
Calvit, Mrs. B.M.	55
Blanton, Dr.	20
McNeel, P.S.	14

<u>Matagorda County</u>

Mills, Power & Warren (Caney Place)	352
Maj. Abram Sheppard	340
Col. P. Hardeman	260
J.B. & J.D. Hawkins	206
Capt. John Rugely	150
Col. Henry Jones	130
Mrs. Ann Thompson	60
Estate of G.R. Kemser	55
Henry Gibson	45

<u>Wharton County</u>

Gov. A.C. Horton	305
Capt. W.J.E. Heard	106
Eli Mercer	80
James C. Meyers	40

<u>Fort Bend County</u>

Johnathan D. Waters	320
Terry & Kyle	300
W.W. McMahan	100

Sugar Production in Texas, 1854
P.A. Champomier

<u>Brazoria County</u>	<u>Hogsheads</u>
Mills, Robert & David G.	1085
Low Wood Place	670
Bynum Place	415
Jackson, Abner	480
Lake Place	160
Retrieve Estate	320
Smith, Morgan L. (Waldeck)	410
McNeel, Sterling (Darrington)	405

Name	Value
McNeel, John G. (Ellerslie)	325
Sharp, W. (Chenango)	320
McNeel, P.D. and Estate of L. H. (Pleasant Grove)	305
Estate of Perry, James F. (Peach Point)	220
Mims, Sara (Mims)	220
Runnels, Hal. G.	220
Manor, William	175
Westall, A.E.	170
Wharton, Mrs. Sarah A. (Eagle Island)	170
Caldwell, James P. (Oakland)	166
Tinsley, Issac J.	160
Patton, C.R. (Patton/ Varner - Hogg)	120
Townes, Judge R. J. (Peach Lake)	120
Sayre, Charles D.	120
Row, Shadrach	100
Bell, T.C. & J.H.	75
Bates, Gen. Joseph	75
Calvit, Mrs. B.M.	65
Hall, W. D. C.	63
Winston, S.P.	50
Yeiser, D.F.	35
Blanton, Dr.	27

Matagorda County

Name	Value
J.B. & J.D. Hawkins	200
Maj. Abram Sheppard	170
Mills & Warren (Caney Place)	139
Capt. John Rugely	100
Mrs. Ann Thompson	28
Henry Gibson (lost crop by storm)	0

Wharton County

Name	Value
Gov. A.C. Horton	260
Gapt. W.J.E. Heard	100
Eli Mercer	80

Fort Bend County

Name	Value
Johnathan D. Waters	315
W.W. McMahan	80

Sugar Production in Texas, 1855
P.A. Champomier

Brazoria County	Hogsheads
Mills, Robert & David G.	1280
Low Wood Place	820
Bynum Place	460
Jackson, Abner	784
Lake Place	133
Retrieve Place	651
Smith, Morgan L. (Waldeck)	460
Estate of McNeel, Sterling (Darrington)	450
McNeel, James G.	312
Jordan, Levy	288
Runnels and Campbell	265
McNeel, P.S. and Estate of L. H. (Pleasant Grove))	263
Manor, William	262
Estate of Perry, James F. (Peach Point)	210
Patton, C.R. (Patton/ Varner - Hogg)	200
Mims, Sara (Mims)	192
Sharp, W.	175
Caldwell, James P. (Oakland)	168
Westall, A.F.	163
Sayre, Charles D.	150
Winston, S.P.	150
Wharton, John A.	130
Townes, Judge R. J.(Peach Lake)	120
Winston, Anthony	104
Bates, Gen. Joseph	100
J.W. Brooks	100
Row, Shadrach	95
Winston, William	90
Tinsley, Issac J.	70
Chirouze Brothers	50
Calvit, Mrs. B.M.	47
Matagorda County	
Mills & Warren (Caney Place)	360
J.B. & J.D. Hawkins	249
Maj. Abram Sheppard	220
Capt. John Rugely	100
Mrs. Ann Thompson	30
Wharton County	
Gov. A.C. Horton	260

Eli Mercer	60
Fort Bend County	
Johnathan D. Waters	460
Terry & Kyle	340
W.W. McMahan	120

Sugar Production in Texas, 1858
P.A. Champomier

Brazoria County	Hogsheads
Mills, Robert & David G.	810
Low Wood Place	450
Bynum Place	360
Jackson, Abner	790
Lake Place	90
Retrieve Place	305
Darrington	395
McNeel, James G.	320
Ellerslie Place	250
Homestead Place -	
Estate of L. H. McNeel (Pleasant Grove)	70
Smith, Morgan L. (Waldeck)	300
Jordan, Levy	250
S. S. Perry (Peach Point)	240
Westall, A.E.	212
Sharp, W. (Chenango)	200
Wharton, Mrs. Sarah A. (Eagle Island)	165
James Campbell	160
Munson, Gerard	160
Mims, Sara (Mims)	150
Estate of Patton, C.R.	150
Bryan, W.J.	150
Townes, Judge R. J.	125
Bates, Gen Joseph	125
Row, Shadrach	105
Winston, F & L	100
Estate of T. J. Coffee	100
Estate of Manor, William	95
Ballinger & James	90
Winston, S.P.	90
Calvit, Mrs. B.M.	85
J.W. Brooks	75

Staton & Cloman	70
Chirouze Brothers	18
John H. Harris	15
<u>Matagorda County</u>	
Mills & Warren (Caney Place)	150
Abram Sheppard & Co.	120
J.B. & J.D. Hawkins	80
<u>Fort Bend County</u>	
Col. Jonathan D. Waters	350
Kyle & Terry	150

Chapter 3:

1. Letter from James Reed to James F. Perry.

New Orleans, 4th May, 1846
    James F. Perry Esq.
        Dr. Sir

    I could not agree to take Jackson's note for the very reason that he has no intention whatever of paying until he is forced by law to do so, independent of this he boasts of the privilege the law gives him. He has made two good crops since I took his note & he has not shown any willingness to appropriate one dollar of the proceeds towards this debt but said to Mr. Butler that the law might take its course.

    Should it not impair my rights in any way, I will request Mr. Butler not to issue an execution against you, hoping at the same time that you will endeavor to discharge the debt and urge Jackson to aid you from his next crop to do so - I have very little confidence however that Jackson will pay you anything and it would be well enough not to plan too much reliance upon any money from that source. - I herewith annex a statement of your note and interest to the 1st of May last which, together with the note annexed you will please sign and return and upon recpt of said note , I will immediately forward you your note for $600.

        Very respectfully

        James Reed

2. Letters from James Hamilton to James Perry from the James F. Perry papers, Courtesy of James L. Smith.

On March 26, 1847, James Hamilton wrote to James F. Perry from New Orleans stating that:

Dear Sir,

    I beg leave to say to you that I have every expectation of obtaining from New York by the 1st June an account equal to lift my every encumbrance on our Oyster Creek Lands. If by some accident anything should prevent this be assured the 1st January will not find me one dollar in arrears in paying off our whole debt.

    But if by the extreme prospect on the money Market in New York we cannot get the Money until, next Winter. You must not disturb Jackson this Summer. Any injury to his credit would event an operation on the Court and might be very injurious to your own interests at San Luis. Indeed Dear Sir you have a great Stake in sustaining a man of his decision and energy in our Enterprise.

                      I remain with esteem
                           Very respectf.
                           Your ob Sevt.
                           J. Hamilton
        Oswichee P.O. Russel County, Alabama

On January 1, 1848 from New Orleans, James Hamilton sent another letter to James F. Perry in care of R & D. G. Mills, Brazoria:

Dear Sir,

    I find with the view of sending on some collateral securities from Charleston (which are under my control) I shall have to repair to that place this Mor to send them here to authorize Majr Jackson To draw to remove the Lien - on the Oyster Creek Property. He will therefore not be able to draw until the 15th or 20th Feby when he will be sure to do so in payment of you [sic] judgment against him.

I remain Dear Sir
        with esteem
                respectfully
                      your ob sev
                            J. Hamilton

A letter from Hamilton to Perry, was addressed to the polite attention of Messrs R & D Mills, and was written on the 12th of February, 1848 from Savannah Georgia:

Dear Sir,
I shall be compelled to go myself to Texas to see that all the Liens are removed from the Oyster Creek Lands which Major Jackson bought of you and Mr. Harris. The attorney genls Certificate is endorsed on the back of the Titles before I can draw for the Money for your payment.

I shall leave Alabama on the 1st March and be at Brazoria on the 15th of the month for this purpose.

3. Marriage Contract between Abner Jackson and Sarah Brownlee.

State of Louisiana
City of New Orleans

This agreement made and entered into (in duplicate) on this twenty fourth day of December, in the year of our Lord one thousand eight hundred and sixty, by and between Abner Jackson of the County of Brazoria and State of Texas of the first part, and Mistress Sarah L. Brownlee of Charleston District in the State of South Carolina widow of Elijah Brownlee late of Charleston District of fore said, deceased, of the second part, who are about to enter into the marriage state and become husband and wife.

That the parties hereto have and do by these presents agree to the stipulations, rules, regulations, and agreements upon which their said intended marriage shall be governed, and which are as follows: to wit:

First: The said partied of the first part shall hold and enjoy in his own right, all the properties which he now or at the time of the celebration of the said marriage shall possess or own, as well as such other property as he may there after acquire by gift, devise, or decent, or by purchase or exchanges with his separate funds or property, and upon the death of the party of the first part, the party of the second part should she survive him, Shall have no interest in his or for life, in any of said property, but when time of said property shall descend to and rest in the children of the said part of the first part, or their descendants, or in default thereof to his next of kin. Subject only to the payment of the debts of the party of the first part and to his right to make any other disposition of the same by last will and testament.

Second: the party of the second part shall hold in her own right all the property which she now possesses or at the time of the said intended marriage shall possess as well as all such property as she may thereafter acquire by gift, devise, or descent, or by purchase or exchange with her own separate funds or property. Said property shall not be liable for any debt or engagement of the party of the first part contracted or to be contracted unless the party of the Second part shall give in writing, (with the consent of the party of the First part.) A Special lien upon the same and upon the death of the party of the Second part, the party of the First part, should he survive her, shall have no interest in fee or for life in any or such property but the whole thereof shall descend to and rest in the children of the party of the Second part or their descendants or in default thereof to her next of kin subject only to the payment of the charges against said property, and to her right to make any other disposition of the same by last will and testament.

Third: The party of the First part, or husband of the party of the Second part shall have the control of all her property.

Fourth: These articles shall remain in force, no matter to what State or Country they may hereafter remove to.

In testimony where of the party of the First and Second here to have here unto signed their names and affixed their scrolls for seals before Daniel B. Ricards, a Commissioner in and for the State of Texas, resident in the city of New Orleans, State of Louisiana, and before two competent witnesses, Joseph Heay and William B. Kimball.

Chapter 4
1. July 1, 1862, Inventory by John C. Jackson of the estate of Abner Jackson.

An estimates inventory of the property belonging to the estate of Abner Jackson, deceased.

4428 Acres of land being the league of land originally granted to D. Tally, together with the sugar house and all other improvements, the plantation which is on said land is known as the Darrington Place.
Value $60,000.

1200 acres of land adjoining the same out of the league granted to Bradley and bought by A. Jackson .
Value $14,700.

The growing crops on the Tally league is estimated as follows,
230 acres in sugar cane $14,500.
335 acres in cotton $5,000.
335 acres in corn $2,000.
54 bales of cotton $2,160
132 Hhds sugar averaging 800 lbs $6,600
4000 bushels corn $2,000.
100 bales cotton in the shed $3,400.
9000 lbs fodder $140.
62 barrels molasses $930.
3 wagons $180.
11 carts $700.
1 Timber ? wheel $75.
79 ploughs [plows] $380
Blacksmith tools $40.

Plantation tools		$191.
5100 [of something - can not decipher]		$100.
1500 head cattle		$9000.
56 mules		$4,200.
15 yoke oxen		$600.
39 head horses and colts		$680.

Total $127,576.

300 heads of hogs $600.

And the following negro slaves:

		$
Margaret	35	600
Andy	18 months	150
Mary	20	900
Mandy	20	900
Maria	39	600
Arcis	19	800
Lydia	2	150
Big Ellen	48	500
Little Ellen	25	900
Emma	2	150
Elizabeth	39	600
Parthinia	5 months	100
Edie	14	700
Francis	20	900
Fanny	60	250
Hannah	60	250
Sally	49	250
Sarah	19	650
Angeline	18	900
Adaline	20	900
Becky	15	900
Louisa	15	900
Lucy Harry	60	250
Little Lucy	22	800
Lucinda	14	800
Viney	39	800
Charlotte	50	400
Caroline	20	900
Cheney	15	800
Devey	25	850
Dliash	18	400

Name	Age	Value
Rose	50	200
Rickter	29	750
Charles	1	150
Rhoda	25	900
Kate	1	100
Jane	50	100
Julia	25	850
Marshall	18 months	200
Parthenoneo	18	850
Palace	14	600
Felix	13	800
Ernest	12	900
Boston	60	100
Armshead	40	900
Adam	16	1000
Bill Jack	35	900
Jim Mitchell	29	1000
Jim Ray	20	1000
Mose	24	1100
Pete	26	1000
Joe	28	1000
Wise	22	1050
Walton	25	1050
Wash	20	1050
Sam	22	950
Henry	26	1100
Little Henry	13	800
Harry	13	800
Daniel	22	1100
Hiram	40	800
Dennis	12	600
Old Harry	50	700
Darse	45	800
Gilbery	32	1100
Charles	32	1100
Old Armstead	60	100
Solomon	100	00
York	100	00
Toney Bluit	16	200
Patsey	44	500
Peggy	60	250
Rhoda	58	150
Andrew	12	800

Dorse	11	700
Tilla	60	000
Emma	70	000
Sylva	55	000
Old Charles	70	000
Elevern	60	200
Levenia	8	400
Sophy	8	450
Pinkey	10	450
Dilsey	12	400
Rhody	12	300
John	10	500
Arie	10	400
Betsey	7	400
Virginia	6	350
Hiram	6	400
Pathe	8	400
Aleck	5	300
Martha	4	250
Dicie	5	250
Ben	22	100

3200 acres of land out of the lands on Oyster Creek, originally granted to J.E. Groce, purchased from L.M. Wiley on the 4th of June 1859.

Valued at $8.[An acre?]

The following named Negroes on the Retrieve Plantation purchased on the 9th day of April 1859 or since that time.

Jim Sunday	40	950
Anthony	38	1000
Benoni	40	900
Middleton	30	1050
Fenney	2	200
Luckey	5	250
Linus	25	1000
Caesar	50	600
Stuart	20	1100
Johnston	22	950
Jake	18	1100
Ben	25	1100
Russ	35	750

Name	Age	Value
Judy Sunday	24	850
Tyre	16	900
Prince	28	1000
Henry	20	900
Jeff	24	1100
Daniel	28	1100
Judy	25	800
Frances	3	300
March	6	350
Clamssa	45	600
Lucinda	10	500
Juno	40	750
Middleton	2 months	100
George	7	400
Eve	40	500
William	6	400
Hager	3	250
Milly	30	900
Butler	6 months	100
Harriet	?	250
Phebe	35	450
Jimmy	14	850
Nancy	5	250
Nessy	40	400
Jenny	8	450
Elsy	45	450
Dave	12	500
Clamida	10	400
Norris	8	350
General	6	300
Eliza	1 1/2	150
Aleck	3	250
Pinkey	50	400
John	8	400
Washington	5	250
Abram	65	100
Henry	100	00
Hager	75	00

1/2 of 52 mules val in gross at	$3900	$1950
1/2 of 3 ponies	$150	$75
1/2 farming utensils	$800	$400
1/2 30 hds Sugar	$2100	$1050

Andrew	1	100
Alice	5	250
Betsy	12	700
Celsy	22	900
Dido	45	400
Daphne	26	550
Dormis	1	100
Sylva	48	200
Lydia	25	850
John	3	200
Sarah	26	850
Pickens	1	100
Curnsy	50	200
Becky	10	650
Nelly	3	200
Polly	100	00
Abby (one leg)	33	100
Malinda	2	150
Liah	25	200
Hannah	100	00

(90 slaves)

38 mules	$1900
6 yoke oxen	$270
about 400 head of cattle	$2400
44 Hds sugar	$3700
89 Bbls Molasses	$1335
35 bales cotton (silk)	$1750
2400 bushels of corn	$1500
4 stacks of fodder	$60
farming utensils	$450
2 wagons	$200
13 carts	$450
100 hogs	$200
25 bales cotton unbaled	$875
2 horses	$60

317 acres growing cotton crop
250 acres growing cane
300 acres growing corn

Estimated and included in the valuation of the Lake Jackson Plantation, consisting of 2544 acres out of S.F. Austin tract and 1200 acres out of J.E. Groce tract, including growing crop as above stated:

$50,000

Household & Kitchen furniture $500

One undivided half of the Retrieve Plantation as originally purchased consisting of 3400 acres out of the Austin grant on Oyster Creek.

Whole place valued at $57,000
Jackson Interest $28,500

The stock of cattle on the Retrieve Plantation containing about 800 head at $6. per head $4,800

Separate property continued 1/2 800 acres of land attached to the Retrieve and bought on the 4th of June, 1859 from J.M. Wiley.
Whole tract valued at $8. per acre, $6,400. $3,200

Recapitulation
Separate property of A. Jackson deceased as noted in the foregoing inventory added up and stated as gross $241,661.00

One half of the property of the community as noted in the foregoing inventory added up and stated in gross as $154,710. $77,355.00

Sum of separate property, interest in community $319,016.00

I solemnly swear that the above and foregoing inventory is a full and complete inventory of the property belonging to the estate of Abner Jackson deceased, so far as the same has come to my knowledge and I have separated as far as I have been able the separate from the community property of said Abner Jackson deceased.
    John C. Jackson
       July, 1, 1862

Chapter 5

1. Slave's work schedule by months from the H. G. Shrock's Plantation Journal of Activities, Wharton County, Recorded between 1860 and 1865; Abner and Margaret Jackson Probate Records; Elizabeth Silverthorne's <u>Plantation Life in Texas</u>; J. Carlyle Sitterson, *Sugar Country: The Cane Sugar Industry in the South, 1753 - 1950* 1953 University of Kentucky Press, Page 112.

January
cleared new fields
chopped cotton and cane stalks
piled cotton stalks
burned cane stalks
cut and raked corn stalks
started plowing fields with mules and oxen
started planting sugar cane
chopped weeds
repairs and additions to buildings
hauled fodder
hauled to market
shelled, cleaned and ground corn
cut and hauled wood
cut and hauled poles
hauled rails
cleaned fence corners in fields
butchered hogs
repaired fences
repaired corn cribs
repaired cotton pens
made repairs to main house
built meat house
repaired horse lot fence
built horse blocks
prepared garden
set out shallots
straightened honey suckle
planted peas, sage, beets, lettuce and mustard seeds
hauled cotton

February
planted sugar cane
plowed and hoed cane
cut briars out of cornfield
cut and burned weeds in fields
burned cotton and corn stalks before the plowers
plowed fields with oxen and mules
started planting corn
cut poles, built pen for garden
worked garden
planted Irish potatoes, beans and peas
plowed potato patch

made potato ridges
ginned & baled cotton
burned trash
fixed fences
butchered hogs
made sausage
hauled wood
worked in blacksmith shop
dug creek bank
hauled cotton to market
spun cotton
shelled & ground corn
repaired cabins
built shed for loom
set up looms
built pen to catch wild hogs
road building
hauled last years corn to the cribs
chopped corn field
shelled seed corn
busted out cotton middles
trimmed off potato beds
cleared timber
cleaned cisterns
fired cane brake
sharpened tools
butchered meat
ditched the yard

March
plowed and hoed sugar cane
plowed fields
raked and burned briars in corn field
planted corn
scared birds off corn
blocked off corn
hauled cotton seed
started planting cotton
raked after cotton planters
harrowed cotton ground
plowed cotton and corn
blocked off cotton
scrapping cotton
broke out middles in corn
shelled last years corn
hauled corn to market

cleaned and ground corn
mended fences
built fences
planted sweet potatoes
repaired wagons
butchered hogs & deer
plowed garden
planted peas, beans, sugar, corn, brown corn, pop corn
and shallots in the garden
ginned & baled cotton
hauled wood
cut & hauled ties & split rails
fence repairs & fence building
cleaned fence corners
fixed cross fence
sharpened tools
repaired bridges
cleared new road to cane break
cut new road to timber
cut and hauled timber
ground corn
prepare potato ridges
hauled cotton to market
repaired gate
repaired wagons
cut board timber
cut bee tree
riving boards
hauled wood
build shelter for horses
made slave clothes
cut timber for cotton hoops
made cotton hoops
made hoe handles
spun and wove cotton

April
plowed and hoed sugar cane
finished planting cotton
planted corn and cane seed
plowed new ground
broke cotton middles
plowed and hoed cotton and corn
blocked off corn
scrapped and swept cotton and corn
thinned corn

chopped cotton
ground last years corn
took corn to market
cut bee tree
spun and wove cotton
made slave clothes
hauled boards and poles
built horse shelter
made bee gums
plowed and hoed the garden
planted broom corn seed, tomatoes, mush melons, cushaw seeds
peas, cabbage, beets, beans and watermelon seeds in
garden
ridged up potato ground
set out potatoes
took cotton to market
killed and slated beef
baled cotton
built cistern

May
plowed and hoed sugar cane
swept and scrapped cotton
hoed corn and cotton
plowed corn and cotton
thinned corn
sweeps in all fields
sharpened tools
repaired wagon
hoed potatoes
worked garden
baled cotton
hauled cotton to market
made soap
ground corn
set out tobacco
hoed peas
ridged potato ground
repaired sweeps
repaired wagons
tended garden
plowed potato patch
hauled coal wood
put up coal kiln
repaired plows
broke out cotton middles

butchered beef
built new chicken yard
cotton blooming

June
plowed and hoed sugar cane
plowed cotton and corn
hoed cotton and corn
sweeps in the fields
hoed potatoes
hauled oats
sharpened farm tools
repaired buggy
made hoes
split rails to make horse lot
hauled wood
dug well
ground corn
hoed oat patch
worked on roads
cut and hauled timber
built horse lot
beat timber for baskets
make cotton baskets (With itinerant basket makers who would stay about a week at each place.)
made cotton sacks
hauled corn
ginned cotton
cut broom corn
picked peas

July
sweeps in cotton
hoed cotton
started picking cotton
ginned cotton
started cutting corn
shucked corn
planted winter corn
repaired fences
cut & split rails
hauled cotton
hauled poles
cut broom corn
picked peas and beans
road work

pulled fodder
stacked fodder
began picking watermelons
ground corn
repaired buggy
hoed potatoes
planted Irish potatoes
fixed gate
hoed new ground
straightened cross corn
fired cane break
planted winter vegetables in garden
cut and hauled wood
made hogshead and molasses barrels

August
picked cotton
set gin
ginned cotton
packed cotton bales
transported bales to market
set potato slips
hoed new ground
fixed fodder stacks
made wagon tongues
repaired wagons
road work
ground corn meal
repaired gin
picked corn
ground corn
worked potato patch
cut and hauled wood
herded mules
hauled fodder for mules
cut bee tree
harvested potatoes
plowed out potato patch
set and fired coal kiln
cleaned out wells
planted cabbage, cauliflower, turnips, mustard and beets in the garden
made hogshead and molasses barrels

September
picked and ginned cotton

bagged cotton
transported cotton bales
took cotton bales, barrels of corn, bundles of fodder and corn meal to market
plowed turnip patch
hoed and picked corn
shelled corn
ground corn meal
hoed second year land
herded mules in corn field
robbed bee gums
shod horses
mowed fields
chopped weeds
penned the cavy yard
cut and hauled wood
made hogshead and molasses barrels
made repairs to sugar mill
cleaned out boilers

October
picked, ginned, and baled cotton
weighed and packed cotton
started cutting cane and processing sugar
hauled corn
hauled bales
chopped weeds
hauled wood
ground corn meal
cut bee tree
split rails
thrashed peas
hauled rails
hauled cotton seeds
killed hogs
raked barley patch
chopped corn stalks

November
picked, ginned and baled cotton
hauled cotton, corn and potatoes to market
cut cane and processed sugar
processed hogs and deer
repairs to structures
cleaned and ground corn meal
repaired chimneys
hauled fodder

split rails
hauled rails
hauled wood

December

picked, ginned and baled cotton
hauled bales to market
finished cutting cane and processing sugar
hogsheads and molasses to market
hauled wood
ground meal
butchered hogs
made sausage
built hen nests
hauled fodder
hauled logs
split rails
made shoes
penned cavyard
Christmas celebration (In December of 1862, John Jackson paid
$62. for six and one half gallons of rum for the slaves
Christmas celebration at Darrington.)

Chapter 6: "Amounts received from Negroes on account of things furnished them off plantation and for board while unemployed and for fines for misconduct and abuse of team and tools during year 1866." Jackson Probates, Folder 6, Item 320

"Amounts received from Negroes "
Robert Strobel (Black) for one mare 32.50 and 1 mule 15.
Noriss Gordan for board 1.50
Ohio McNeel for 1 mare and 1 colt 32.50
Daphine Jackson for board and docked for refusing to work 42.40
Samuel Jackson for board and use of stock ect. 30.00
Myess Brown on board and forfeits 23.30
Shadrack Jackson for board 27.00
Sam Mills for one horse 40.00
Chaney Mitchel for board forfeits 6.50
Jim Mitchell for horse, saddle, and board 41.13 and 63.00 and 22.87
Maria Mitchel for board 13.00
Gabella Small board 2.00
Rhoda Mitchel board 4.00
Debby McNeel board 3.00
Halston Knight for lost time 26.00

William Navigan for horse/old 19.15
Earnest Daniel for mare   29.62
William Fields [payment] on mare 24.35
Wise Wood [payment] on horse   50.50
Sam Willis on lost time (amount not given)
Frances Mitchel for board, forfeitures, etc. 6.50
Andrew De Costor for lost time etc. 11.00
Andrew Paine lost time etc. 8.00
Monday Pickney for horse, board, etc. 68.00
Abram Ferrel [payment] on Horse, board etc. 40.00
Sancho Robertson [payment] on mare   35.00
Pate Mitchell (Mitchel) [payment]on mare   37.50
Samuel Tucker board   1.00
Angie James board   1.00
Amanda Austin board   2.00
Mary Payne board   1.50
Juda Day   board   1.00
Julia Bingham for board etc. 6.00
Mary James 1 horse and board 36.00
Monday Small 1 mare   30.00
Hamp Woods for use of mule   3.25
Joe Green for 1 saddle and board   6.00
Walton Payne for board and lost time 13.50
Lizzie Small for board and lost time 5.50
Louisa Austin board and lost time 8.25
Daufney Jackson board and lost time 6.00
Dan Wood Jr. mare   27.50
Santana Gordon   board and fines 13.00
Henry Burney board 1.50
Dan Woods   fine for riding mule 15.00
Charlotte Johnson board 1.50
Douglas Winters board 1.00
Thomas Jenkins lost time, fine and board 17.50
Dennis Groce for 1 mare, fines etc. 55.00
Agenarzo Goffany   lost time 17.50
Mosy Bolen lost time   3.33
Aaron Bolen lost time 3.33
Samuel Colier   lost time 3.33
Total collected from Negroes $949.94

www.ingramcontent.com/pod-product-compliance
Lightning Source LLC
Chambersburg PA
CBHW080336170426
43194CB00014B/2586